ARBARIANS

rst staged at the Greenwich Theatre in September 1977,
arbarians is a trilogy of short plays concerning the fluctuating
ortunes of three school-leavers, two white boys and one black.
n the first play, *Killing Time,* they are all unemployed, hanging
bout the streets, drifting into petty crime. In *Abide With Me,* a
ear later, the three are stranded, ticketless, outside the walls
of Wembley on Cup Final Day, their frustration building to a
savage climax. A further year passes and in the final play, *In the
City,* set during the Notting Hill Carnival, the two white boys
are looking for a 'final fling' before one of them has to leave on
a tour of duty in Northern Ireland. The third member of the trio
turns up, having 'made good', and disappointment, fear and
tension flare into fierce racial hatred.

Though deeply serious, *Barbarians* is often also hilariously funny,
because so accurately observed. As Time Out said of *Killing
Time:* 'Keeffe's vital writing keeps its concern within deftly
accurate character portraits, but his humour relieves the
desperation of the kids' situation.'

'Of all the new playwrights who have emerged during the past
few years, Barrie Keeffe strikes me as the one with the most
authentic voice. His plays mirror his time with absolute veracity.
He is concerned and compassionate, reporting what he sees, and
offering no glib explanations or doctrinaire solutions.'

Frank Marcus, *Sunday Telegraph*

'It captures unerringly and with unhistrionic force a sense of life
down in Lewisham where unemployment is running rife and
demoralisingly among the bored young. . . it is not a grim play
though the final implications are chilling. There is a raw and crude
humour in the situation and language of these unemployed boys
. . . it is magnificently a play of today.'

The Guardian (on *Killing Time*)

'nerve shattering . . . it makes Peter Terson's *Zigger Zagger* seem,
in retrospect, like a Sunday School outing'

Daily Telegraph (*b Me*)

D1513838

by the same author

In Methuen's Modern Plays
GIMME SHELTER
A trilogy of short plays:
Gem, Gotcha and Getaway
A MAD WORLD, MY MASTERS

In Methuen's New Theatrescripts
BASTARD ANGEL
FROZEN ASSETS
SUS

The photograph on the front cover shows Karl Johnson,
Philip Davis and Elvis Payne in the Soho Poly production of
Abide With Me *and is reproduced by courtesy of Nobby Clark.*
The photograph of Barrie Keeffe on the back cover is by Tony
Bock and is reproduced with permission.

Barrie Keeffe

Barbarians

A trilogy comprising
Killing Time, Abide with Me
and In the City

EYRE METHUEN · LONDON

*For the Soho Poly, and
all who work there.*

First published in 1978 by Eyre Methuen Ltd,
11 New Fetter Lane, London EC4P 4EE
Reprinted in 1981
Copyright © 1978 by Barrie Keeffe
ISBN 0 413 38990 1

Set IBM by 🇫\Tek-Art, Croydon, Surrey.
Printed in Great Britain by Fakenham Press Limited,
Fakenham, Norfolk.

Contents

Note:
Cuts were made in both *Killing Time* and *Abide With Me* for the
Greenwich production — these cuts were made to reduce the
length of the evening and are indicated by brackets. The cuts are
not necessary if the plays are presented individually as one-act
plays. However, there are lines in all three plays that should be
cut if the plays are presented alone. These lines are indicated by
* before the first word to be cut and * after the final word to
be cut.

Barbarians was first produced as a trilogy at the Greenwich Theatre, London on 29 September 1977 with the following cast:

PAUL	Nick Edmett
JAN	Karl Johnson
LOUIS	Jeffery Kissoon

Directed by Keith Hack
Designed by Voytek

The following music was used for the Greenwich production:

Before *Killing Time*	*Career Opportunities* by The Clash
After *Killing Time*	Sex Pistols' *Anarchy in the UK*
Before *Abide With Me*	Sex Pistols' *Pretty Vacant*
After *Abide With Me*	*Police and Thieves* by The Clash
Before *In The City*	The Jam's *In The City*
Curtain Music	Sex Pistols' *God Save The Queen*

The setting throughout was a brick and corrugated iron wall covered with graffiti.

KILLING TIME

A play in one act

The first part of BARBARIANS

Killing Time was first produced by the National Youth Theatre at the Soho Poly Theatre Club, London on 22 August 1977 with the following cast:

PAUL	Michael Kelly
JAN	Robert Glenister
LOUIS	Dotun Adebayo

(Shane Anderson played Misog and Ashley Burns the chauffeur; these two characters were cut for the Greenwich production and have been cut from this text).

Directed by Bill Buffery

Lights up on an empty stage: the back wall smothered with ripped posters and graffiti. Old bits of newspapers on the floor, discarded cigarette boxes and coke cans.
JAN, 16, is doing a handstand against the back wall.
Music fades.

JAN. Life is a shit sandwich. The more bread you've got, the less shit you have to swallow.

Pause. PAUL, all nervous energy, older, comes on. He sees JAN, hesitates, then runs at him and kicks away JAN's hands. JAN falls.

Whatcher do that for?

PAUL. I felt like it.

JAN. Just minding me own business standing upside down . . .

PAUL. You look more of a prick on your feet than your head.

JAN. England makes more sense upside down.

PAUL. How did it go?

JAN. Oh, it was another wank.

PAUL. I told you not to go. Why humiliate yourself?

JAN. Gotta go, ain't I.

PAUL. To be humiliated?

JAN. Guess who I saw there?

PAUL. Half the class from last year.

JAN. Apart from them . . . outside the Job Centre, guess who I saw?

PAUL. Fucking Prime Minister.

JAN. The career's officer, from school — remember him?

PAUL. The bloke who kept pissing his trousers?

JAN. Yeah him.

PAUL. At the Job Centre?

JAN. An', see, I see him and I twigged it, didn't I? He's on the fucking dole, in't he? They give him the elbow. Now he's on the fucking dole.

PAUL. Loverly. They offer you anything?

JAN. Tin Box Factory.

PAUL. You tell him what to do with it?

JAN. I said, 'I ain't having that. It's all fucking bints, in't it.' He says: 'You bent?' I says, 'I ain't fucking doing a bint's job.' I said: 'Choosey, ain't I.'

PAUL. Should have shot the bastard.

JAN. Yeah.

PAUL. There's another forty thousand leaving next week. An' still they ain't got nothing for all us who left last year!

JAN. Deaths.

PAUL. What?

JAN. A lot died, in the year.

PAUL. Yeah.

JAN. If 40,000 died every year —

PAUL. Yeah?

JAN. Be all right, wouldn't it?

PAUL *sniffs, paces.*

PAUL. When you get killed in a car smash, you come. Cousin told me.

JAN. How's he know?

PAUL. Breakers yard, got a job in a breakers yard.

JAN. Get you in?

PAUL. Nar, it's gone broke. He said: car smashes, write-offs, they're full of spunk. You shoot it all over the windscreen.

JAN. I don't believe it.

PAUL. He found a penis in a writ-off Cortina. The ambulance man must have forgot to put it in his little plastic bag. Me cousin said it had lipstick marks round the top.

JAN. Wow.

PAUL. Geezer went through the winder, head first.

JAN. What a way to go! I never knew that. I wouldn't mind a breakers yard.

PAUL. Me cousin would have had me like a shot. At the yard. But he went down.

JAN. I know.

PAUL. When he come out, the geezer he'd left in charge, this geezer had sold off all the gear and legged it. To Canada. To be a Mounty. Me cousin was all for getting off after him. Things he was going to do to him. He was gonna hatchet him. Chop off his prick with a pair of rose pruners. Me old man talked him out of it.

JAN. Good.

PAUL. He said, 'Come off it Keith. It just ain't on. I mean, it just ain't on. You piss off to Canada and chop the prick off a fucking Mounty.'

JAN. Right.

PAUL. You kidding?

JAN. What?

PAUL. Really, the career's officer?

JAN. He told me. I said, 'What you doing here then?' He said, 'I'm on the fucking dole same as you.'

PAUL. That's rich. Me mum's going up the wall.

JAN. Taken a photo?

PAUL. She's up the spout again . . .

JAN. Does your dad know?

PAUL. He said he did it.

JAN. Did he?

PAUL. How the fuck should I know. Think he must've. He hit her when she told him.

JAN. Cunt.

PAUL. Not hard. Still . . . not the thing to do is it. It ain't exactly love story at the flicks. 'Dwarling, we're gonna have a baby.' Wallop round the head. I mean, that ain't exactly — not Hollywood.

JAN. Nar, nor's a lot of other things. You've got to get out. Get a room.

PAUL. Gonna get a flat ain't we!

JAN. You ain't mentioned it.

PAUL. Well, need the old bread first right. As soon as one of us gets a fucking job . . . right . . . get a flat.

JAN. O good. What's tonight then?

PAUL. Car spotting, in't it.

JAN. What's he want now?

PAUL. Wants a Rover 3,500.

JAN. Eh?

PAUL. You heard. Ideally like — left hand drive.

JAN. There's no Rover 3,500s round here. Fucking left hand drive!

PAUL. French order.

JAN. Fuck that. I mean, left hand drive Rover 3,500s ain't exactly thick on the ground in Lewisham, are they?

PAUL. Try up town. Newer the better.

JAN. Tonight?

PAUL. Phone him soon as we see one . . . he's got the geezers standing by. Hyst it tomorrer and strip it in twenty-four hours. Be in France Saturday.

JAN. Left hand drive though.

PAUL. That's ideal. Don't matter. Come on, few quid. Something to do anyway . . . only otherwise killing time ain't we?

JAN. Right. How we get up West End then?

PAUL. Louis, he'll have some bread . . . for the fares.

JAN. Yeah.

PAUL. Sister leaves him a quid under the mat outside the door. Leaves the light in the hall on.

JAN. I'd poke her, I ain't fussy.

PAUL. He'll just be pissing around somewhere. If she's got a geezer in. And he'll have a quid . . .

JAN. There he is, wanking again.

Lights off and suddenly up on LOUIS *who speaks directly at someone in the first row of the audience. He holds Whitehouse magazine.*

LOUIS. One night the bleeding bulb had gone, hadn't it. In the hall. I gets back, no light on, so I goes in don't I and there she

is with her skirt up round her waist on the mat in front of the
telly and this great white hairy arse pumping up and down on
top of her. I'll give 'em their dues, they didn't get put out
like. Nar, she just starts having a go at me don't she. She says,
'What the fuck you doing in here?' I said, I says: 'I come in
for me tea, ain't I.' She says, 'Get out willya.' Still this great
hairy white arse up and down, up and down. He don't even
look at me, does he. I says, 'That's nice in't it. I got more
rights to come in here and have me tea than you have to be
doing that.' I mean, there's a time and place for everything
ain't there. And Match of the Day's on the tele, Millwall.
Jimmy Hill doing a slow motion replay bit how this bloke
got it from the narrowest of angles and I thought: You're
fucking telling me! I was a bit pissed 'cause I'd had this bit
of luck with a parking meter like and I'd had this half bottle
of Johnny Walker see and just sits there and the guy goes
Errrrrr. Flakes out, looks up, hadn't even noticed I'd come
in. Looks round, it's the fucking geography teacher ain't it!
He says, 'You cunt.' I says, 'That's nice – in me own home,
like.' This is when I was at school, weren't it. Next day, makes
me do five mile cross country, don't he! Says I'm athletic
don't he. Fed up people saying I'm athletic. Anyone tells me
I'm athletic – I know they're trying to con me. He says I
could be an Olympic sprinter. Be a British hero he says, in
the Moscow Olympics. Yeah, British hero in Moscow. In
Lewisham I'd still be a bloody nigger.

Looks at magazine.

LOUIS. I wonder if it's the *same* Whitehouse?

*Now JAN and PAUL are either side of him. PAUL snatches
the magazine.*

PAUL. All this wanking Louis son.

LOUIS. I weren't wanking.

PAUL (*quietly*). Too much wanking makes your ears go funny.

LOUIS. Pardon?

PAUL (*shouts*). I said: Too much wanking makes your ears go funny.

LOUIS. O.

JAN. Does your sister fancy me?

LOUIS. Nar, you're on the bleeding dole. She only likes boys
with money.

PAUL. Teachers!

LOUIS. History teacher last night. This rate she'll go through the whole staff room and when I was there I never been inside it.

JAN. Saw the careers teacher on the dole.

LOUIS. On the dole!

PAUL. He's on the dole, they give him the elbow.

LOUIS. Serves him right. He never knew what he was talking about. He was the one who —

JAN. I know, I know.

LOUIS. He said, go on this government training course.

PAUL. He told everyone that. You was the only stupid prat who believed him.

LOUIS. Refrigeration, he said train in that. He said everything'll be frozen soon. He said it's the coming thing. He said go on the training course, they guarantee you a job if you do the year's training. Did the whole bloody year. I'm an expert in refrigeration.

JAN. Yeah, all that.

LOUIS. I could freeze anything. If I had something to freeze. If I had the equipment and the tools, I could turn me hand at any sort of refrigeration job. Pity there ain't none.

PAUL. You got the quid then?

LOUIS. Nar not tonight, she ain't got no-one up there tonight.

JAN. What's up with her?

LOUIS. Me mum's home ain't she.

PAUL. Lost her job?

LOUIS. Nar, no cleaning tonight . . . they got a do up there ain't they. Banquet, ain't it.

JAN. You what?

LOUIS. There's this do up there — so the cleaners did it this afternoon. Mum arf nicked a lot of fags — here have one.

They all light cigarettes.

What the thing is . . . look.

PAUL (*reads brochure*). 'The Mayor's Banquet will be served with a variety of European wines and as in other similar

banquets the loyal toast is to be drunk in the words of
Dickens with all due enthusiasm . . . smoking before the loyal
toast is considered a serious breach of et. . . eti. . . eti. . . quat.
And this rule is never relaxed although on rare occasions the
loyal toast has been proposed earlier than usual to suit the
comfort of a very distinguished guest, such on one notable
occasion President Eisenhower. . . Tonight's guest of honour
will be Mr R.W. Kershaw, the Borough's Youth Employment
Officer.

JAN. With musical entertainment by Bob Marley.

LOUIS. You're joking — honest?

PAUL. Fuck off.

LOUIS. She's going up there early in the morning. . . after they
have banquets up there, the fucking food they chuck away.

PAUL. Counting on fare from you to get up town for a motor.

LOUIS. I'm fed up spotting motors for your cousin. Costs more
spotting them than he pays us for phoning him.

JAN. You got a better idea?

Pause.

LOUIS. What motor?

JAN. He wants a left hand drive Rover 3,500.

LOUIS. Left hand drive — I've never seen a left hand driver, not
a Rover 3,500. Not in Lewisham.

PAUL. That's why we wanna go up West in'it. Hotels.

LOUIS. What's he want a left hand drive for anyway?

PAUL. Frenchman.

JAN. They drive left handed on the Continent.

LOUIS. Bloody mad. One of Sylvie's boyfriends was gonna go to
Spain in his motor, weren't he. And Sylvie's other geezer
says they drive on the other side of the road over there. So's
next week he comes round and Sylvie was thinking he might
take her with him to Spain and he says, 'Nar, I ain't going.
This driving on the other side of the road lark. I tried it on
the South Circular last night and it's fucking murder.'

PAUL. Daft Spade.

LOUIS. He weren't a spade, she never goes with spades . . . she
hates black blokes, she says they've never got no money.

JAN. Don't matter if it ain't left handed. That was preference.

PAUL. Tell you what . . . lot of motors outside Tiffanys. Have a butchers at Tiffanys like?

JAN. Come on . . .

LOUIS. All right, I'll come with you then.

JAN. His mum's up the spout again.

LOUIS. Again, blimey! Must be something they put in the water at your flats.

PAUL. That's all I need. Another fucking brother.

JAN. Let's take a butchers at the motors at Tiffs.

JAN *and* LOUIS *retreat and* PAUL *addresses the audience.*

PAUL. I think he did it deliberate, like giving her another one to tie her down. They was cutting back and they stuffed him on the night shift, like. On the night shift at his age. He didn't fancy it, but they was cutting back, see. Thought he'd keep her out of mischief so give her another one. Gonna seem funny, calling a bleeding baby a brother. He tried to get me in there, but they was cutting back. It's all been a waste of bleeding time since . . . I can't remember when it weren't a waste of bleeding time. School was a waste of bleeding time. Everything was boring. This careers bloke kept rubbing it in, he kept saying he did, future is in your hands, he said. Yeah, yeah . . . like trying to catch a fucking Frisby in the wind. He was right panicked all the time. Tell you the truth, I felt sorry for the bloke, I did. Dashing about trying to fit people up and he knew, and we knew and *he knew we knew* that it was all fucking hopeless, but it's hard to imagine. He said once, he said . . . look here, he said, imagine Wembley, cup final . . . all them people, hundred thousands he said. Right, imagine that. He said that's how many school-leavers have been on the dole for more than a year. So he says, you've got to make yourself presentable ain't you, make yourself presentable, get in there, get stuck in. Tell yourself you ain't gonna be one of them. So's what did I do, I bought a suit didn't I. Fucking suit. For the interviews. Traipsing round all keen at first, so's I wouldn't be one of them and . . . I give it to brother when he got married. Eight quid seventeen, a week. I was better off when I did the milk round when I was at school. I was buying records then, I bought an album most weeks. Spot the motor for me cousin, be a few quid . . . no trouble, at Tiffanys . . .

Flashing coloured lights downstage and music: Status Quo. Loud at first then fading down so we can hear them speak. They face the audience in a straight line; the audience is the foyer of Tiffanys. Just JAN and LOUIS.

JAN. All in their lovely clothes.

LOUIS. At least rocker girls show a bit of leg.

JAN. Yeah.

LOUIS. They wear stockings. At least with rocker girls, you can see up their fucking skirts.

JAN. Stupid looking Teds. And their bints look fantastic.

LOUIS. Me sister had a Ted once.

JAN. What, Sylvie had a Ted?

LOUIS. Yeah, she says you gotta try things when you get the chance. She said it took him about a half an hour to get his bleeding drainpipes off.

JAN. We're never gonna find a left hand drive Rover round here.

LOUIS. Now if it was a left hand drive Cortina . . .

Pause.

JAN. What?

LOUIS. I never seen a left hand drive Cortina in Lewisham neither.

JAN. Have to go up West for the Rover, have to be right hand drive.

LOUIS. Well, right hand drive Rover — there's hundreds. That's no problem. See I've been thinking it had to be left hand drive, that's why I weren't really looking. Never get a left hand drive —

JAN. You say everything three times.

LOUIS. Eh?

JAN. You say the same thing three times.

LOUIS. Yeah, well boy — I gotta lot of time on me hands. Dead cinch finding a right hand drive Rover.

PAUL comes on.

PAUL. Not a fucking Rover in the car-park, not a Rover in sight.

LOUIS. I was just saying —

PAUL. What?

LOUIS. You ain't gonna get a left hand drive Rover, not here.

PAUL. Go up West, the hotels. Good chance there. I mean, he said right hand'll be all right.

LOUIS. O well, that'll be all right.

PAUL. Anything. Bloody waiting list. Pay a grand over the top for a new Rover 3,500. There's a lot of fucking money about.

LOUIS. Yeah, you should see the things me mum's been bringing home from the charring — bloody leg of ham.

JAN. She'll get done sooner or later.

LOUIS. Nar, it's all right. They put her in charge of security ain't they. She has to look in the other women's bags don't she . . . that's when she does the nicking. Her and the security guard bloke. Leg of ham size of . . . size of . . . for this banquet. The Mayor's Banquet.

PAUL. Ain't seen you flashing it.

JAN. Yeah, well . . . went off in the heat didn't it. I could have refrigerated it, could have . . . if I'd had the equipment and a fucking refrigerator. I could freeze anything, given the equipment and a refrigerator. I'm an expert, mate. When I left the training course, the teacher he says: 'You're an expert in refrigeration.' I was right chuffed, first time I've ever been called an expert. He said: 'Refrigeration is the same in any language.' Think someone would have wanted a refrigeration expert. Bloody funny that. A whole year —

PAUL. He fucking goes on.

LOUIS. Yeah, boy — watch it. You're talking to a refrigeration expert.

PAUL. One kick with the right boots and this whole winder'd go in.

JAN. And the bouncer'd strangle you.

PAUL. Nasty bastards. No Rovers in the car park. Have to go up West . . .

JAN. Yeah. Got any money though?

PAUL. Forty p.

LOUIS. Forty p, that all you got?

PAUL. How much you got?

LOUIS. O . . . yeah well . . . I got thirty-five.

JAN. I wouldn't mind going in there . . . hang about, have a couple of pints, you know.

LOUIS. Yeah.

PAUL. I had a shifty. Fire exit's locked, in't it. Stupid thing to lock a fire exit. Supposed to be open so you can get out in a fire.

LOUIS. What about —

PAUL. What?

LOUIS. What about, we set a fire in there and then they'll open the fire exit and we can get in?

PAUL. You prat.

JAN. What's the point of going in if it's on fire?

Pause.

LOUIS. O yeah.

PAUL *talks directly to a girl in the front row of the audience.*

PAUL. You fancy me, don't you?

JAN. She's looking at you.

PAUL. Whatcher!

LOUIS. She's looking away. Leave off, you're embarrassing her.

PAUL. Don't blush, if you played your cards right you could have me.

JAN. Wouldn't play snap to have you.

PAUL. I'm all yours. If you can lend me the money to get in. Ain't got-no-money so they won't let me in. (*Pulls out pockets to show and coins drop.*)

LOUIS *smiles at the girl, strikes a moody pose. Cigarette dangling from lips.*

PAUL. Fucking James Dean of Lewisham. Ain't it never occurred to you . . . you can't be James Dean. He was white.

LOUIS. That was on the outside. O Christ, I wanna see them movies again. When they're on somewhere. I wouldn't mind getting killed in a car crash. If I had a car, what a way to go.

JAN. Rebel without a car.

LOUIS. Before I get a car though . . . get a leather jacket like, and this white T-shirt like, and some winkle picker cowboy boots like and come up here, won't I —

JAN. When's this?

LOUIS. Oh, when I gotta job and got some money, like. I'll come up here, lean on the bar, you know, in the corner, hunch me shoulders up like, squint a bit like — see, he was short sighted — so I'll hunch me shoulders and lean against the corner of the bar dead moody and rebellious like, right mysterious like, and they'll all think: Who's that dark mystery man who looks just like James Dean?

PAUL. Have the car smash after?

LOUIS. Well, not if I've pulled anyone. Wouldn't like to smash up me Porche if I've got this bint in it with me who's mad about me, you know.

JAN. That's very decent of you.

LOUIS. Wouldn't want to kill her and all. I wonder if you know when you're dead? I wonder if the dead know they're dead?

JAN. I'll ask 'em at the factory.

PAUL. The factory?

JAN. If I went, I mean.

PAUL. Bint's job — that ain't a job for a geezer, in a factory with bints.

LOUIS. They trying to get you to go there — the factory with the bints?

JAN. Don't miss a fucking thing do you?

LOUIS. I turned that down. Not gonna do a girl's job am I?

PAUL. No way, that's right. Not a girl's job.

JAN. Nar . . . but, did think . . . just to fill in a few weeks like, something to do, bit of proper money. . .

PAUL. No way, it's not on.

JAN. Nar.

LOUIS. Tell them what to do with it.

JAN. Yeah, I did.

PAUL. What did he say?

Pause.

JAN. He said . . . 'Fussy, ain't you.'

PAUL. You stay fussy. Stick to your entitlements.

JAN. Right.

LOUIS. Stick to your entitlements, that's what I say.

PAUL. You bet.

LOUIS. Just see meself in a factory with bints. I'm an expert in refrigeration. Done the year's training.

JAN. I ain't.

LOUIS. Shows I weren't a prune then, don't it.

PAUL. I got it. I got it. Tell you where there's a good chance there'll be a bloody Rover 3,500 — why didn't I think of it before. You know where they all go with their flash cars, to screw, on the flats, by the duck pond . . . fucking in the open on the flats.

JAN. Right.

PAUL. Go and spot the motor there, give me cousin a buzz — tenner each in.

LOUIS. Right.

JAN. Good thinking, Batman.

PAUL. That's where me cousin took his bints before he got his own place. In the motor. Have it off by the duck pond. Straight out of the Young Tories . . .

JAN. Eh?

PAUL. Used to go to the Young Tories' dances, didn't he. Said Young Tory bints, fuck like rattlesnakes, don't they. If you've got the readies. Go like rattlesnakes.

LOUIS. I wonder if Margaret Thatcher was a Young Tory . . . when she was young?

LOUIS *and* PAUL *exit, laughing.*

JAN (*to audience*). His cousin's got it all sussed out. . . since he's been out. Great bloke, his cousin. Really smart . . . they're really close. Gonna have Paul in his business with him, when Paul gets his licence. He can supply anything. . . Tell him the motor you want, he'll get it for you. Like waiting list for new Jags — there's no waiting list with his cousin. Rovers, great!

Every new model, he's laughing. Every strike, he's over the moon. He bungs us thirty quid for spotting the one he's after . . . If they can afford the motors, serves the bastards right when they have 'em nicked. That's what his cousin says. Must be nice, to have a cousin like that . . .

The THREE *leaning against the back wall; half light.*

JAN. E Type . . .

LOUIS. Audi, Audi — lot of Audis about.

PAUL. And. . . would you believe. . . Rover 3,500.

LOUIS. No way that's gonna be left hand drive.

PAUL. I tell you, that was only ideal.

JAN. Fantastic.

PAUL. Yeah, but how long's he gonna be there?

JAN. Half an hour . . .

LOUIS. Depends, don't it.

PAUL. No good.

JAN. Latest registration — dead right.

PAUL. How's he gonna nick it if the geezer's sitting in it, you clown?

JAN. O yeah.

PAUL. Parked car! Stupid idea, coming here.

LOUIS. Could have been up West by now.

JAN. Wait a minute, wait a minute . . . they're getting out.

LOUIS. Hot night, in't it.

PAUL. Fucking in the open, disgusting, pervert.

LOUIS (*shouts*). Perverts.

PAUL (*clasps hand over* LOUIS's *mouth*). Shut up, idiot.

JAN. Idiot.

Pause.

PAUL. So's what we do . . . make it right easy, extra tenner . . . what we do . . . when he drops his pants, right . . . finger the keys outa the pocket, right. They'll have to go home on the bleeding bus — ring me cousin, hand him the keys when he gets here to drive it off. Well, what d'yer say?

Pause.

PAUL. Okay then Louis?

LOUIS. Ah, come off it . . . I ain't going over there and picking his pocket while the geezer's on the job. What you take me for?

JAN. You're used to it — be just like home.

LOUIS. Leave off . . . it's one thing phoning up your cousin telling him we've spotted a motor. It's another thing nicking keys in't it.

Pause.

In't it?

PAUL. Chicken.

LOUIS. I ain't chicken.

JAN. Well, do it then.

Pause.

LOUIS. Why me? It's your cousin.

PAUL. I gotta phone him, ain't I.

LOUIS. I'll phone him.

PAUL. You don't know the number.

LOUIS. Tell me then.

PAUL. My contact, in't it.

LOUIS (*to* JAN). You do it then.

JAN. You're more athletic than me.

LOUIS. Every time something blows out, someone tells me I'm athletic. I ain't athletic.

JAN. It's getting dark, he'll never see you coming.

LOUIS. 'Course he'll see me coming.

PAUL. Not if you lay on the floor . . . wriggle along, you know, like a snake and that . . .

LOUIS. And pick the bloke's pocket?

PAUL. Right.

LOUIS. While his trousers are round his ankles?

JAN. That's it.

LOUIS. On top of the bird?

PAUL. }
JAN. } Yeah!!!

Pause.

LOUIS. I got me best trousers on.

PAUL. So what?

LOUIS. I might get dog shit on them.

PAUL. Extra tenner, be worth it.

LOUIS. Say he sees me . . . he'll think I'm a bleeding pervert meself.

JAN. Hammer him.

LOUIS. Suppose he shouts help?

PAUL. I'll be right behind you, kick him one, and we're off.

LOUIS. Bloke on the job, turns round and sees my face and my hand going down his pockets . . .

PAUL *begins to walk away.*

PAUL. That's it, finished with you. Come on Jan.

JAN. Yeah, he's chicken.

PAUL. Just see James Dean chickening out of —

LOUIS. You leave Jimmy out of this!

PAUL. He'd do it like no-one's business.

LOUIS. I know he would.

PAUL. Well then!

LOUIS. Hmmmm. (*Scratches his head.*) All right then. I'll do it. But the extra tenner's mine then?

JAN. Okay.

PAUL. Yeah, it's a deal.

LOUIS. And you promise not to tell no-one?

PAUL. No way.

LOUIS. 'Cause it's criminal. I don't wanna be a criminal. I'm a qualified refrigeration expert; all I need is a criminal record, ruin me career before it starts.

PAUL. That's the deal.

LOUIS. Okay then. Here goes. (*He gets on the floor.*) Hope there's no snakes.

JAN. No snakes.

LOUIS. This heat, this heat they start hatching right poisonous snakes. Just be my luck, poisonous snake bite me balls off.

He wiggles.

PAUL. Okay then . . . before he's got going . . . those old geezers it's all over in two minutes.

LOUIS. How do you know he's old?

PAUL. If he can afford a Rover 3,500, he fucking must be.

JAN. Go on then.

LOUIS. I'll just slide down there and nick his keys then.

PAUL. Have a look in the ignition first . . . make sure he ain't left them in the ignition.

LOUIS (*leaps up*). Wish you'd make up your mind! Okay then. (*Down again.*)

Pause.

And you'll be right behind me?

PAUL. Yeah.

LOUIS. If he gets nasty — you'll be right behind me.

JAN. We will.

LOUIS. Okay, ta ta.

LOUIS *slides off.*

JAN. He's on his way.

PAUL. He's athletic, in't he.

JAN *sits on floor smoking.*

PAUL *addresses the audience.*

PAUL. Cousin, he says — it's all a con. All a con, know what I mean? He's a great con-man. Started on the milk round first of all, like. Learned a lot. Didn't bother with housewives and that. Robbing his own class. Shops like, he'd make about sixty

quid a week. On the fiddles. First week, he'd go short
himself . . . say charge twenty crates instead of twenty-one.
Next week, charge for twenty-two. If they spotted it, he'd
say, 'last week I did meself short.' And he could prove it.
If they don't say nothing, proves they ain't checking, so he
sticks at twenty-two. Never get too greedy. . . just a tenner a
week. Each shop. I was in the boozer with him one night and
this geezer comes up to him, manager of a little supermarket.
Geezer says to my cousin: 'You cunt. You was doing me a
tenner a week for years.' Cousin right embarrassed — see by
then he'd moved on from the milk round . . . Geezer said . . .
'I didn't mind you doing it, you kept it in decent proportions.
But this new bloke, he got too greedy, so I told him to piss
off. His fiddles was getting in the way of me own racket.'

JAN. Louis is taking his time.

PAUL. Better get them keys . . .

JAN. Yeah . . .

PAUL. Me cousin bought a Jag. Gear he wears now. House he's
gonna buy. Near a park, for the golf like. Only way.

JAN. You'll work for him?

PAUL. Later . . . get a licence, be a driver for him. Screaming
along the motorways. Cross channel ferry in the middle of the
night. Drop off the motor in Paris or where have you and
home for tea. O yeah, when I get me licence.

Pause.

When I get me licence.

Enter LOUIS *jangling keys.*

LOUIS. I got 'em!

PAUL. You got 'em son?

LOUIS. 'Course I got 'em, course I got 'em, I said I was gonna
get 'em, I got 'em. Didn't I. Here.

Tosses keys at PAUL *who catches them, rejoicing.*

PAUL. He got 'em.

LOUIS. I got 'em.

JAN. Great.

LOUIS. Great — I was fantastic. Easy. Like greased lightning,
way me fingers went. His arse going up and down, up and

down. Terrible it was, pong. He kept farting.

PAUL. What?

LOUIS. And belching and farting. Fart, belch, fart, belch. Blimey
— the bint, she must've bin deaf and . . . what d'yer call it
if you can't smell?

PAUL. Dunno.

LOUIS. That and all. I was great — where was you? You says
you was gonna be right behind me, right behind me you said
in case he got nasty, in case he saw me.

PAUL. I knew you'd do it, knew I could rely on you.

LOUIS. Having a fag — me getting farted at by this great hairy arse.

JAN. Have a fag.

LOUIS. I'll have one me mum nicked from her place. O shit (*He
takes out cigarette packet. It's crumpled.*) Look.

JAN. Have one of these.

LOUIS. Tar. I could make a fortune picking pockets.

PAUL. Easy, in't it?

LOUIS. Dead easy. If you wanted to do it, I mean. But only if
you wanted to do it. I ain't gonna start thieving. Down the
slippery slope, that is — no stopping.

JAN. What?

LOUIS. That's what the careers teacher said at the training
course. When I was training to be an expert. Good on you
son, he says. Get trained up, then there's no risk of being on
the dole and sliding down the slippery slope.

PAUL. All that.

LOUIS. That's what pisses me off.

JAN. What?

LOUIS. Being all trained up and still on the fucking dole.

PAUL. Phone me cousin.

PAUL *goes and* JAN *hands* LOUIS *a match.*

JAN. Have a light.

LOUIS. Yeah, that's nice. Need a fag after that. She was right
young.

JAN. Yeah?

LOUIS. Right pretty.

JAN. Was she? *Me Uncle Harold says there's nothing like a flash motor for pulling young bints.*

LOUIS. I think she was a bit pissed off with the belching farter.

JAN. Well, you would be, wouldn't you.

LOUIS. Beautiful motor . . . what a motor . . .Oh, I'd arf like a motor like that.

JAN. Louis.

LOUIS. What?

JAN. If you hadn't done your training course —

LOUIS. I wouldn't be a refrigeration expert, would I.

JAN. If you hadn't done it, and the dole, for the whole year — and at the dole they said about — like, taking this job, in the factory . . . with the bints, like . . .

LOUIS. Yeah?

JAN. Would you?

LOUIS. Oh, well . . . gotta stand by your entitlements.

JAN. After a year though . . .

LOUIS. Well . . . why?

JAN. See.

Pause.

LOUIS. What?

JAN. I took it, didn't I.

Pause.

LOUIS. What, the job in the factory with the bints?

JAN. I said, I said — yeah.

LOUIS. You must be mad, boy.

JAN. It was seeing the bleeding careers officer on the dole, weren't it. Threw me, didn't it. I dunno . . . and never having no money — just temporary like, only till something proper comes up like.

Sudden smashing of glass.

PAUL *appears kicking glass and staggers towards them holding a telephone on a lead which he has ripped out of the kiosk.*

PAUL. Cunt.

JAN. What?

PAUL. Cousin, phoned him . . . said . . . got the motor . . .
said . . . got this lovely sparking, shiny new Rover 3,500 —
and, added bonus, I said — we nicked the keys I said.

LOUIS. I hope you told him it was me who nicked the keys.

PAUL. And he says . . . says, says he don't want a fucking brand
new Rover, wants one of the old ones, the old posh ones, like
what the olduns drove — he wanted a fucking old one.

JAN. Oh, fuck it.

PAUL. Fucking liberty . . . fucking laughed at me didn't he. I
thought he'd —

Pause.

Thought he'd be really impressed . . . nicking the keys,
thought he'd . . . thought that'd right impress him, nicking
the keys.

LOUIS. Your eye's bleeding.

PAUL. When I kicked in the phone kiosk . . . (*He tosses away the
receiver.*) Think a bit of glass went in me eyeball . . . can you
see it?

JAN. Nar . . . Christ . . .

LOUIS. Won't see it here . . . under the light.

PAUL. Aw fuck it, maybe it's a gnat or something . . . stinging.

JAN. It's bleeding . . . must be glass.

PAUL. Gnats bleed, don't they.

LOUIS. O yeah, if you hurt it — a gnat'd bleed. Everything bleeds,
if you hurt it.

PAUL. Fucking stinging . . . fucking cousin . . . fucking car.

LOUIS. I was just saying to Jan here, I was saying — that bloke,
talk about fart. He farted and belched the whole time he was —

PAUL. Yeah, well — he can go and fart and belch his way
home . . . give us them keys again . . .

LOUIS. In me pocket, why —

PAUL (*he takes keys.*) Chuck the fucking keys in the fucking
duck pond. Let him walk home, fat arsed prick.

He throws the keys off. Splash.

JAN. Yeah, serves the bastard right.

LOUIS. I nicked them.

PAUL. Yeah, well — that motor's no good to me cousin.

LOUIS. I might have got attacked when I was —

PAUL (*screams*). Wrong motor. (*Quiet.*) Wrong motor, weren't it . . . (*Pause.*) All he did was . . .

JAN. What?

PAUL. He laughed.

Silence.

Hope he has a bloody long walk.

LOUIS. Yeah, serve him right.

JAN. Yeah.

LOUIS. I'm going home then.

JAN. Waste of fucking time. Again.

LOUIS. Oh. (*Rummaging in pockets, inspects keys.*)

PAUL. Let's go home.

LOUIS. Hang on, hang on. O no, I don't believe it.

JAN. What?

LOUIS. Fucking keys you chucked in the duck pond . . . wrong fucking keys. They was my keys.

JAN. How do you mean?

LOUIS. These are the car keys.

JAN and PAUL fall about laughing.

Ain't funny!

PAUL. So what? Your mum's in anyway, kick the winder in and get in. Bleeding eye . . . right stinging, you sure there ain't . . .

JAN. Get in the light.

LOUIS. Nar, that don't matter but they was me mum's keys . . . her work key's on the ring . . . for the security . . . they was her keys you've chucked in the duck pond.

PAUL. Wait a minute, you telling me . . . all night you've been walking round — and in your pocket, the fucking keys to where your mum works, where they're having the Banquet, where she knocks off all great legs of ham and fags and fuck knows what — that what you saying?

LOUIS. Chucked her keys away, yeah.

PAUL. Shit . . . we could have been up there, knocking off some of the booze and . . . could have gone up West, spotted a motor and . . . you cunt.

LOUIS. Don't call me that. You gotta be careful who you call that. Bloke might turn out to be fucking Kung-Fu champion or something.

PAUL. You ain't.

LOUIS. No, course I ain't . . . but I'm just warning you in case you said it to someone who was.

PAUL. Get them fucking keys . . . get them and up to where your mum works and knock off something . . . won't seem like a waste of time then.

JAN. Yeah.

LOUIS. Gotta get them back for the morning . . . for her.

PAUL. Come on . . . Feels like a fucking needle in me eye . . .

Darken stage. Sound of splashing about in water.
In the darkness we see the three lads with trousers pulled up to their knees and holding matches, lit to see with.

LOUIS. This is ridiculous.

JAN. Shut up and keep looking.

LOUIS. What if there's lizards or crabs in here?

PAUL. They didn't go to the middle . . . keys only round the edge here . . . I was right pissed off they never got to the middle.

JAN. Something . . . nar, just a bit of metal.

LOUIS. This is really stupid . . . really stupid.

PAUL. You're the stupid bastard . . . telling us all about the knocked off legs of ham . . . knocked off fags . . . walking round with the fucking keys in your pocket . . . what else does she bring home?

LOUIS. Some booze . . . she brought some champagne home . . . saving that for Sylvie's wedding.

PAUL. She getting married?

LOUIS. Will one day.

PAUL. Who'd marry her?

LOUIS. You'd be surprised.

PAUL. Surprise me.

LOUIS. Hello . . . bloody bat! Jesus, bloody bat —

PAUL. Ain't a bat you prick. Pair of knickers caught up in the trees.

LOUIS. Thought it was a bat.

JAN. Is it a bird, is it a plane — no it's —

ALL. Batman.

They hum the Batman theme.
Then after two times, LOUIS sings.

LOUIS.   Batman,
          Hanging on a lastic band
          Fell into a pot of jam
          Along came Spiderman
          Thought he was a bogey man and
          Ate him!

They laugh.

Sing that to me brother's baby. Right likes me singing that.

JAN. Be able to sing it to your baby brother.

PAUL. Yeah . . .

JAN. Shh . . .

Pause.

LOUIS. What?

JAN. So quiet . . . never heard it so quiet . . .

They listen.

PAUL. Here . . . down here . . . thought it was here somewhere, by this sign . . .

He holds up the keys, with the other hand he holds his eye.

JAN. Fantastic!

PAUL. Here, catch Louis —

He throws a stone. LOUIS dives and a great splash.

LOUIS. You stupid arsehole!

PAUL. Nar . . . that was a stone . . .

PAUL *jangles the keys.*

LOUIS. I'm soaking in mud, ain't I.

JAN. Be a fast runner . . .

PAUL. Dry off . . .come on . . . get up there in that geezer's
motor . . .

JAN. Hey, get dressed . . . get a move on . . .

JAN and PAUL splash off. LOUIS strikes a dramatic pose.

LOUIS. All mud and slime . . . smothered in mud and slime . . .
like Jimmy . . . there's this scene . . . in Giant . . . when no-one
don't wanna know . . . see . . . don't wanna know and he's on
his own and no-one wants to know, takes the piss outa him
and then he finds oil don't he, on this bit of land, like . . .
and they're all sitting there, all these people who take the piss
out of him 'cause they think he's a right wank . . . and there
they are, sitting in their posh clothes on the . . . outside the
house . . . and they see him coming . . . and he's all smothered
in oil . . . he looks right black, looks like a black . . . all oil all
over his face and hands and clothes . . . and he stands there
arms up, like a gladiator or something . . . and he just looks
at them, he just looks . . . whites of his eyes staring . . . cause
he fucking knows . . . fucking knows what they think of him
. . . but now, different now . . . he's fucking got 'em. I
liked that bit. Liked that bit.

He does his James Dean look at the audience.
Sound of a car starting off.
LOUIS hesitates, then runs off.
Blackout.
Sound of end of God Save The Queen.
A triangle of light floods out from an open door off.

VOICE. And now, my lords, ladies and gentlemen . . . the loyal
toast. Be upstanding and raise your glasses. Her Majesty the Queen.

VOICES. Her Majesty the Queen.

Applause.

VOICE. And now, to address this banquet . . . our most
distinguished guest . . . Our Youth Employment Officer,
Mr R. Kershaw . . .

Applause.

*Out of the doorway comes JAN with a crate of wine. Then
PAUL with his arms full of champagne, brandy and whisky*

bottles. Then LOUIS *with a leg of ham and a huge chicken.
They hold fingers to lips. All this very silent. They set the
stuff down stage centre.* JAN *and* LOUIS *return to the room.*
PAUL *opens a champagne bottle. Fizz and bubbles. He gulps
it down.*

During this . . .

VOICE. My lords, ladies and gentlemen . . . A time for
rejoicing, a time for celebration. But this year, the usual end
of term pleasure in our schools will have been overshadowed
by the tragic statistics of youth unemployment — something
that rightly and properly is being described as the most worrying
social problem of the 'seventies. The fact of the matter is,
there are now 253,379 school-leavers on unemployment
registers in the United Kingdom and as the school year did
not end in some parts of the country until after this month's
count was taken, the figures in August will be still worse. But
the problem of youth unemployment is not confined to
those who left school this summer; there are now more than
100,000 youngsters who have now been unemployed for
more than a year and this month's figures will include many
more who are destined to accompany them along this
depressing and potentially destructive path to adulthood . . .

By now JAN *and* PAUL *have come out with more bottles.
They all have one open and sip from champagne and switch
drinks, getting drunk very fast.*

PAUL. Shut the fucking door then . . .

LOUIS *shuts the door and we only hear a murmur of speech.*

JAN. So much gear —

PAUL. Just getting chucked away.

LOUIS. So much, they'd never notice some is gone . . .

PAUL. Jesus, this bleeding eye.

JAN (*looking*). Can't see nothing . . . oughta get up the hospital
with that . . . in case it is a bit of glass. . .

PAUL. Stopped bleeding, anyway.

JAN. Put all this in the motor and drive it home . . . flog it.
Easy eh?

LOUIS. I dunno about that . . . dunno about that . . . that's criminal.

PAUL. Right!

LOUIS. I don't wanna blemish me career.

PAUL. What fucking career? You ain't got one.

LOUIS. I'm trained.

PAUL. Trained for what? They just got you outta the way for a year you prick.

LOUIS. But I'm trained though . . . ain't I.

PAUL. This is lubberly . . . lubberly bubbly.

JAN. It rhymes.

PAUL. Rhymes . . . I foresee a great future for meself . . . get this in the motor . . .

JAN. Same motor . . . say the cops is looking for it though . . .

PAUL. Fuck the cops . . . yeah, maybe . . . another motor . . .

LOUIS. Hey, hey hey hey . . . look . . . it's an old one . . .

JAN. Bloody Rover 3,500 — old one.

LOUIS. Ain't left hand drive but . . .

PAUL. That's the one, that's the one . . . how handy . . . how convenient. That's exactly the one me cousin wants . . . and a little Union Jack on the bonnet . . . how pretty . . .

JAN. I'm starving . . .

LOUIS. Chicken here . . .

JAN. Bit of that . . .

PAUL. Bit of that scotch . . . nick that motor . . . drive it up the fucking wall . . . that's what I'd like to do.

JAN. Get pissed, throw up over them snobs in there . . .

PAUL. Open up the motor . . . bung the stuff in there . . . O great.

LOUIS. Looks so nice and shiny . . . black and —

PAUL. Yeah well — soon have all that paint off . . . new numbers . . . new engine number and . . .

LOUIS. Looks very polished and looked after . . . pity it's gonna —

PAUL. What?

LOUIS. Well, get — you know.

PAUL. Sod that . . . get the stuff and . . .

They get the stuff, then turn and pause.

JAN. Shit.

PAUL. Getting in it.

LOUIS. Posh sods.

PAUL. Bloody bloke with a bloody lavatory chain round his neck.

LOUIS. Daft geezer with him . . .

JAN. Bloke from the fucking job centre, in't he . . . bloke who said I'm choosy . . .

LOUIS. They're going . . . car's going . . .

Sound of the car moving away.
They make V signs.

JAN. What we gonna do with all this then?

PAUL. Chuck it back in through the winder?

LOUIS. I could refrigerate this. If I had the tools and equipment.

PAUL. Yeah, all that.

Pause.

LOUIS. Take what we can carry then?

PAUL. Yeah, take what we can carry.

JAN. And . . . not take the other motor?

Pause.

PAUL. I'm too pissed to drive. Might drive it off the bleedin' road and we'll all get killed. Like Jimmy!

LOUIS. Yeah. If he hadn't got killed, he'd be nearly fifty now.

JAN. Fat.

PAUL. Bald.

LOUIS. Nar, he'd still be a rebel!

JAN. Take what we can carry then?

PAUL. On the tube.

LOUIS. Yeah, better than getting killed.

JAN. Right.

JAN and PAUL exit with bottles, legs of ham etc.

LOUIS. Yeah, us getting killed. What a fucking waste that'd be.

LOUIS exits with his arms full of champagne bottles.
Fast blackout, music loud.
End of play

ABIDE WITH ME

A play in three scenes

The second part of BARBARIANS

Abide With Me was first presented by the Soho Theatre Company at the Soho Poly Theatre Club, London, on 28 September 1976, with the following cast:

PAUL	Karl Johnson
JAN	Philip Davis
LOUIS	Elvis Payne

Directed by Keith Washington
Designed by Vivienne Cartwright

Scene One

The sound of a soccer crowd roaring and singing.
Lights up on an empty stage: a corrugated iron wall, rubbish on the floor.
JAN runs onto the stage in full tribal costume — Dr Martin boots, army trousers rolled to the knees, thin braces, no vest, waistcoat, and scarves tied round his head and dangling from his wrists and waist, like a pirate. He leaps up and down — trying to look over the wall.
Pause.
He paces, then — enter PAUL.

PAUL. Well?

JAN. No . . . no joy yet.

PAUL. No joy, what do you mean no joy? Nothing?

JAN. No.

PAUL. Is that what you're saying? Are you saying you blew it? Are you saying: 'I fucked it. It's all a blow out'? Tell me Jan, son — what are you trying to say? I mean — what are you saying?

JAN. No joy.

PAUL. Oh Christ, oh fuck it.

JAN. I did me best.

PAUL. Best, ha. What about your Uncle Harold?

JAN. Ah well —

PAUL. Ah well my arse.

JAN. I reckon me Uncle Harold. I reckon our chances with me Uncle Harold.

[PAUL. I reckon your Uncle Harold is all sat down nice and comfy with a bottle of scotch and his chicken legs by now.

JAN. Nar.

PAUL. And that only if your Uncle Harold managed to stagger past all the hundred-odd pubs on the way without collapsing into a drunken stupor on the pavement.

JAN. If he could find a bloody pub open. Bastards, closing all the pubs.]

PAUL. You and your Uncle Harold between you have — you pair have really fucked it.

JAN. You ain't done so hot.

PAUL. I put a lot of faith in you, Jan, son. I believed in you. I had — faith in you. 'Jan won't let us down'. I've been telling everyone that all week. ['You won't get into Wembley without tickets', they kept telling me. I said, 'Maybe no chance if I weren't going with Jan. But Jan and his Uncle Harold — irresistible combination', I said. 'I wouldn't be surprised if I don't end up sitting next to Callaghan and Mark Phillips and tonsil teeth herself', I said.]

JAN. I did me best.

PAUL. Yeah. Your best.

JAN. This is a good spot here. We can see right down Wembley Way. If we keep looking, we're bound to see me Uncle Harold.

PAUL. Only a hundred thousand people pouring down Wembley Way, son. And a few extra thousand like us who ain't got tickets. How we gonna catch sight of your Uncle Harold from here, then?

JAN. His hat. I saw his hat. We'll spot his hat from here. I saw it on Thursday night. About a four foot top hat, red and white stripes with a couple of red and white balloons on top.

PAUL. Fantastic.

JAN. If you see a bloke strutting down Wembley Way who looks about ten feet tall, that's me Uncle Harold. That's our tickets, Paul.

PAUL. He's got three quarters of an hour. He'd better have them.

JAN. He won't let us down.

PAUL. I've heard that before.

JAN. He won't.

PAUL. We'll see.

JAN. He's great for tickets. Fantastic.

[PAUL. So far, that has not been confirmed by my personal experience.

JAN. For the semi-final he had two tickets for the directors' tea-room. I saw 'em. He showed me them. He said, 'Jan son, I'd very much like to give you one of these tea-room tickets.'

PAUL. Yeah?

JAN. He said, 'Jan, I'd really like to give you one and come in for a cuppa with me and Matt Busby. And all of them. The high and mighty of Old Trafford. But — unfortunately it's spoken for.'

PAUL grins savagely.

He said, 'I've already promised this tea-room ticket to the bloke who flogged me the cost price carpets I fitted in Lou Macari's bungalow. Otherwise, it'd be yours.' I was right choked.

PAUL. I'd have choked your Uncle Harold.

JAN. But, see, it's all long-term planning. By taking the cost price carpet bloke in for a cuppa with —

PAUL. The high and mighty of Old Trafford —

JAN. 'That way', says me Uncle Harold, 'I'm assured of similar favourable cut-price carpet transactions thus enabling me to acquire additional tea-room tickets for future matches which I shall then pass on to you,' he said.

PAUL. I don't want a ticket for a cup of tea! I want a ticket for the fucking final. The climax of the season . . . this memorable, monstrous season. To see U-ni-ted smash to pulp those country bumpkins of poxy Southampton. Christ, there'll be more goals behind that wall this afternoon than — even the bloody Mirror says you'll need an electronic calculator to keep up with the score. On the telly last night they said it'd be the first final to reach double figures since they wore braces and shorts down to their ankles. I gotta see it, I gotta see it. I gotta see it.

JAN. We will, don't worry. Me Uncle Harold won't let me down. Or me mates.

PAUL. He'd better not.]

JAN. He's got enough and more besides.

PAUL. How's that?

JAN. The players — the players' perks.

PAUL. Liar.

JAN. Listen, in the last couple of weeks he's fitted a carpet for Alec Stepney's bedroom and let Gordon Hill have a twenty-five foot length for his sun lounge less than cost price. 'I lost money,' he said. 'I lost money on the deal — for you and your mates.' He said. Great carpets and all. So that they can walk about the house with no shoes on . . . to gently manipulate their feet. They showered him with tickets, out of gratitude.

PAUL. I believe it all. When I've got the ticket in me hand, when I'm inside.

JAN. Maybe Louis —

PAUL. He's taken his bloody time. We said meet here.

JAN. Fancy working on cup final morning.

PAUL. On *the* cup final morning. Teams'll be coming out in half an hour . . . O Christ.

PAUL. I gotta be there . . . fucking hell, ain't missed a match all season . . . Eight quid on train fares every other Saturday . . . eight quid on fares just to see the home matches . . . every bloody match I've seen and when it comes to *the* match, the bloody final . . . oh Jesus. Gotta see them, Doc's Red Army . . . marching out . . . gladiators . . . lush emerald turf . . . band playing . . . sun beating down . . . shining on the Doc's bald spot . . .

JAN. Me Uncle Harold said he's had a hair transplant.

PAUL. I suppose your Uncle Harold fitted it cost price. Behind here . . . fifty yards away . . . the bloody goalposts. (*He beats his fist on the wall.*) Behind this wall . . . if it weren't for this wall . . . Smash it down . . .

JAN. Don't worry, we'll get in. I feel it. The main thing is . . . we're here . . . on the day.

[PAUL. Yeah.

JAN. Drink in that atmosphere . . . I wish cup finals was at night . . . the atmosphere at night matches . . . sixth round at Molineux . . . that Wednesday night . . . fucking felt it . . . throbbing . . . and I thought they'd had it.

PAUL. Two dozen — nothing . . . always come back, never give up . . . like ants . . . they can cross mountains . . . stamp on them, crush them, and they just keep coming, teeming at you . . . I knew we'd win . . . I felt it . . . in me blood . . . bubbling . . .

JAN. I'll never forget that night . . .

PAUL. Weren't a bad night in Sheffield . . . after the Derby match . . .

JAN. Jesus. Don't know how I come to be holding that copper's hat . . .

PAUL. If they'd seen it!

JAN. Chucked it out the window.

PAUL. All that and . . .

JAN. It'll be all right, I tell you. And we're here.] Wembley on the day. Better than watching it on the telly. It wouldn't be the same.

PAUL. That's true. It wouldn't be the same. Mind you, it wouldn't be a bit fucking bad . . . actually seeing the match.

JAN. Uncle Harold won't let me down.

PAUL. Matter of fact, I've got my doubts about your Uncle Harold. I started wondering about him when he painted his house red and white stripes.

JAN. He said it's the only house in Ardwick red and white stripes.

PAUL. I believe that.

JAN. See it from the end of the street.

PAUL. Hardly . . . unnoticeable.

JAN. Neighbours went mad.

PAUL. Think it was bleeding ice-cream parlour.

JAN. It were just after he painted it me Auntie Elsie left him.

PAUL. Ha.

JAN. She said, 'You care more about Manchester United than me.'

PAUL. Ha.

JAN. He said, 'I care more about fucking Stockport County than you.'

PAUL. If Louis uses his loaf . . . on his way up . . . the touts and that.

JAN. Didn't see none.

PAUL. There must be touts. What's his name, Flash Sid or something — get tickets for anything, he says. There was this article in the paper about him. Frank Sinatra, Royal Box at Ascot . . . When there was that farting about, Princess Margaret, you know, and the Queen says to her, 'You'd better piss off for a bit, ducks.' And Margaret says, 'Nar, I wanna see Wimbledon. The final like.' So the Queen says, 'No chance, I ain't having you in the Royal Box with me, scandal you've caused.' But come the Wimbledon mens' final, there was Margaret — sitting in the front row of the Royal Box. Queen right annoyed. She says, 'How'd you get here?' Margaret says, 'Flash Sid touted a ticket for me.'

JAN. Really?

PAUL. Fuck off.

Enter LOUIS, *breathless. Also in tribal clothes.*

JAN. You took your time.

LOUIS. Trouble I've had.

PAUL. Aggro?

LOUIS. No, not that. Bloody mum — hid me bloody Dr Martins didn't she.

JAN. What? (*He laughs at* LOUIS's *fancy shoes.*)

LOUIS. Hid me Dr Martins. When I got back this morning, to get changed — she'd been through me bedroom. She thought there was going to be a lot of aggro today, and — scatty cow — she hid me boots.

JAN. Bit bloody strong.

LOUIS. An' she'd gone out. Out the way. These are killing me. Bought them for Sylvie's wedding — only worn 'em once. Well, we got them?

PAUL. Bit of . . . a hold up.

JAN. Haven't seen me Uncle Harold yet.

PAUL. Much happening tout-wise?

LOUIS. I only saw one and —

Pause.

I feel right stupid without me Dr Martins. I'll kill her when I get home. If she's chucked them away —

PAUL. This tout?

LOUIS. He only had one.

JAN. You got it!

PAUL. To be on the safe side, Louis, mate.

LOUIS. He didn't have three. He only had one.

PAUL. You got it?

LOUIS. No . . . no I never got it.

JAN. As an insurance, we said if we got offered one — get it, we can always flog it when Uncle Harold —

PAUL. Louis, son — why didn't you get it? How much did he want? A hundred quid? A grand? A bleedin' Concorde in part exchange?

LOUIS. Well, see —

PAUL. Did you see it?

JAN. Hold it in your hand?

PAUL. Feel it between your fingers?

LOUIS. There was only one — there's three of us.

JAN. We could have tossed for it.

LOUIS. But —

JAN. Gone Hickory Dickory Dock for it.

PAUL. I could have practised me Kung-Fu on you for it.

LOUIS. It weren't like that.

PAUL. I'm surprised touts have the neck to try it for the Red Devils — the Stretford End Mob, mate — they'll turn his skin inside out and his feet'll end up where his ear-'oles are.

LOUIS. What I'm saying though — he weren't such a bad bloke.

PAUL. A tout?

JAN. Me Uncle Harold said they're leeches. Vampires. Sucking all the goodness out of the game for a fast buck.

PAUL. He should know all about that.

LOUIS. What I'm saying is, he weren't such a bad bloke. Not like a proper tout. See, he had two tickets. One for himself and one for his son. Only last night, his son had to go into hospital. Appendicitis. So this bloke said, he only wanted cost price for his son's ticket. Him being a United fan. He said he didn't want to blaspheme his ideals and the sense of occasion.

PAUL. He what?

LOUIS. And I had it in me hand and . . .

Pause.

JAN. What, Lou?

LOUIS. There was this other kid . . . with his uncle . . . and this kid had come from Australia. To see the final. And so this bloke, who was flogging his son's ticket, he was just about to flog it to me and he sees this kid crying. Coz he didn't have a ticket. And so he says to him, 'Where do you come from son?' And he says, 'Johannesburg.'

JAN. That ain't Australia.

PAUL. Bloody South Africa, ain't it.

LOUIS. He says, 'Johannesburg.' And his uncle says, 'All them thousand of miles. He's a great United fan,' the uncle says. 'I send him the Manchester Evening News and the programme every week. And he comes specially, and he can't get a ticket.' So the fellah says, 'I'll give you me son's ticket. For nothing.' And this kid, he can't believe his luck. He just starts howling again. With happiness. And the fellah says to me, 'You don't mind me giving it to him, do you? 'Cause he come from further than you.' So he took it. And went.

Pause.

PAUL *and* JAN *look at each other.*

JAN. His mum nicking his Dr Martins has affected his fucking head.

PAUL. Great son, great. Fantastic. Very decent of you. Highly appropriate that.

LOUIS. The kid had never seen United play –

PAUL. We spent about five hundred quid this season, travelling the bloody country watching them, getting them here – and you give away a bloody ticket to a geezer that ain't never seen them play!

LOUIS. I was a bit confused. All the excitement and bustle down there. And I've never met an Australian from Johannesburg before.

PAUL. No wonder they wouldn't let you join the Army.

LOUIS. Hey-a, they would have done. I almost did. They wanted me. The recruiting officer would have had me like a shot if it was up to him.

PAUL. And you hadn't failed your intelligence test.

LOUIS. That weren't the reason.

JAN. Shit.

LOUIS. I didn't fail it, anyway. I just . . . didn't get a satisfactory mark. That's all. There's a helluva difference between failing and not getting a satisfactory mark.

PAUL. After what you've just told me, I tell you — I'll sleep a lot happier from now on knowing you never got in the Army mate. Just see you, face to face with the Russian invading Army — you ask them where they've come from, they say, 'Moscow', and you say, 'Help yourself kiddo, seeing you've come from so far.'

[LOUIS. That weren't funny. It all happened so fast, I was confused. One minute I had it in me hand and the next . . . I cocked it up.

JAN. Don't worry Louis, I'm sure me Uncle Harold won't let me down.

LOUIS. Anyway, I can't talk Russian.

JAN. They all talk English. Everyone talks English.

LOUIS. You should hear me old man. He don't.

PAUL. No mocking the Reds. This situation, us here, stranded like — this come-about wouldn't come about in Russia.

JAN. Wouldn't it?

PAUL. Tickets for everyone there. Everyone. Say like, if Moscow Dynamo gets to the Cup Final, right. What they do, the Commies, the Commies go round everyone's house in Moscow and they say to them: 'Do you want a ticket for the final?' If they can prove they're a regular Dynamo supporter, that is. They say, 'Yeah', and the Commies get them all to stick up their hands, all of those that want to go to the final and then, say if Dynamo's playing . . . some other mob or other, well, they goes to where this other team hangs out and they say to everyone there —

JAN. Providing they can prove they're a regular supporter —

PAUL. Of course. Goes without saying. They say, 'Stick up your mits if you wanna see the final,' so they all sticks up their mits and they get counted and then they all get tickets. Very fair that. Only the true fans get in. None of this dishing out

tickets left right and centre to Princess Anne and her bloody
hand-maids and horses and what have you and women who
don't know a football from a blown-up Durex.

LOUIS. What happens if more Commies want to see the final
than can get in?

Pause.

PAUL. They build a new stadium.

JAN. Christ, that's rich.]

LOUIS. And still they're pouring in . . . look at them . . . I
never seen so many people. They can't all get in. When all the
Stretford mob who ain't got tickets turn up . . . oh Christ,
Paul — they'll storm the gates, smash 'em down, pour
in, hundreds and thousands of us. We can all sit round the
greyhound track.

PAUL. You ever stormed a gate, mate?

LOUIS. Nar, but —

PAUL. But, but, but, but. I tried that at Upton Park when they
locked us out. O yeah. Very happy experience that was.
'Storm the gates,' some bastard at the back hollers. They
stormed the gates all right. I was the bastard at the front. Me
nose buried in the gate like a bleeding woodpecker. They
want to storm the gates let them . . . follow them in, at the
back. That's what I'll do. I ain't no battering ram.

JAN. Don't worry, it won't come to that. Uncle Harold won't
let me down. Did you see anyone in his hat?

LOUIS. Ah, well — there was this bloke by the station with a
big red and white top hat . . . so I asked him if he was Uncle
Harold only I couldn't remember his name then, so I said:
'Is your house red and white stripes?' He said, 'No but me
budgies are.' Turns out he was Southampton. Cunt.

PAUL. That's Southampton for you. Bloody yokels, bloody
all cowhands and shepherds and that. [It's very odd a team
that don't come from a big city. Dirt and grime and factory
chimneys. It's unnatural.

JAN. I hate Ipswich. All that bloody fresh air. No wonder no-
one can play there.

PAUL. Ipswich ain't bad. I mean, compared to Southampton,
Ipswich's like bloody Birmingham.

LOUIS. I hate Birmingham.

JAN. Wouldn't mind Francis though.

PAUL. He wouldn't fit in. Not the new style. Not the go go go. Mind you, if we changed styles, if we wanted Francis, he'd come like a shot. He'd take a drop in wages to play for United.

LOUIS. Who wouldn't?

PAUL. These cunts at Southampton. Bloody Channon and —

LOUIS. He's good.

PAUL. He ain't bad, be okay if he played for a city team. But he's got a farm or something. Slows him down. Everything's so slow then, see. You do everything so slow when you're on a farm, it gets into your system. Unless Channon joins a big city club, he's finished.

JAN. Look what happened to Osgood.

PAUL. Proves me point. Now Osgood weren't arf bad at Chelsea. Bit of a fairy, but, not bad. Goes to Southampton — last time I saw him, every time someone pushed a ball through for him to chase, he stood thumbing a lift. He won't get a kick all afternoon.]

LOUIS. See 'em coming up Wembley Way. Load of wankers. No loyalty. Like on a day out. Don't mean nothing to them.

PAUL. Yeah well, don't let that deceive you. Nasty bastards living around the Dell. Year we come up, bloody herded through from the station to the ground we were . . . like bloody sheep . . . cops shoving everyone. Step into the road to get out of the crush and the cops hammered you. Oh, it felt great. They was fucking shitting themselves. I felt — fantastic.

JAN. Was there any —

PAUL. No . . . no bother at all . . . just the look of us stopped that . . . like Denis Law, you know . . . just his look, how it used to be . . . way he stood there, with the net bulging, hands up . . . chin out . . . fucking worship me, slaves, get on your fucking knees . . . and all the defenders scattered about, hating the cocky bastard, yet nothing they could do . . . 'cause it was just the way he looked.

LOUIS. I wish I'd seen Law.

JAN. You ain't seen nothing if you ain't seen Law.

LOUIS. I wish I started coming with you a season earlier, then I'd have seen him.

JAN. I don't know how he could have joined City . . . I don't understand that . . . [Christ Almighty, I even went to bloody Southampton once, to cheer on bloody Southampton 'cause they was playing City. Five quid that trip . . . without the beer money . . . screaming for wankers like Paine and bloody gongly Davis . . . hoping they'd tank City . . . Bloody City won three-none.]

LOUIS. I wish I'd seen Law . . .

PAUL. Oh, you never saw nothing if you never saw Law. So cool. I happened to be in the dining-car with old Lawy once . . . coming back from Burnley I think it was . . .

JAN. I'm glad they're down, I hated that trip.

PAUL. Twenty quid . . . Anyway, I was in this dining-car, like . . . and the waiter was right nervous, 'cause he was serving the King . . . shaking the waiter was, this one dishing out the peas. 'Peas, sir?' he asked Lawy. 'Just a few,' said Lawy, Scottish voice, you know. Like Rod Stewart tries to put on. Then the train goes through this tunnel and rattles about, come out the dark and the waiter's dropped the whole great bowl of peas on Lawy's lap. Now Paddy Crerard or Besty would have lipped him, right? Not Lawy. He just turns round and goes: 'Waiter, I said just a few peas.'

They laugh.

JAN. Bit different from coming back from Millwall . . .

PAUL. Oh Christ, I'll say. Couple of years ago this was, Lou . . .

JAN. Coming up from Division Two.

PAUL. Week before, Millwall mob had really gone on the rampage . . .

JAN. At Bristol.

PAUL. Everyone in New Cross shitting themselves . . . we were nice and quiet . . .

JAN. 'We're the best behaved supporters in the country.' Sang it all the way from the station.

PAUL. Cops frog-marching us . . . keeping us apart . . . then they started chucking stuff — rocks, cans of blue emulsion paint . . . blue hair I had for a month . . . bright blue. I had to wear a bloody hat all the time.

JAN. They started saying . . .chanting, they started their chant . . . all hell broke loose . . . they started chanting . . . 'Munich 58', 'Munich 58', 'Munich 58'.

PAUL. Shits. All them that died . . . I bleeding cried all night . . . and then I'd never heard of Duncan Edwards . . . remember me old lady came into me bedroom. Me and Pam was just waking up . . . me mum howling and she don't give a fart about football . . . she was holding the Daily Mirror and eyes all red and she said . . . 'They're dead. Busby's babes. They're dead.'

Silence.

Just saying it now . . . feel the shivers going through me . . . bloody dead . . . broken bones and . . . Pam started crying, just a kid . . . in the same bed as me . . . I held her as she cried . . . and I swore, I did . . . when I left school, an' had the money . . . I'd do anything, go anywhere, die, if necessary, for that club . . . for Manchester United.

Pause.

JAN. Understand Lou?

LOUIS. Yeah . . .

JAN. And Matt, Matt in hospital — saw the newsreel on telly when he retired . . . sitting up in his hospital bed, eyes full of tears, saying, 'We start again.'

Pause.

He's a great bloke.

PAUL. The greatest.

JAN. Bit old now but —

PAUL. Bit old, but — great bloke.

JAN. Me Uncle Harold said, when he was in the tea-room with him —

PAUL. What?

JAN. He said, 'Matt Busby is a great bloke.' He said, 'He's a saint.'

PAUL. That is a compliment, coming from your Uncle Harold. He'd know all about saints.

JAN. I know he won't let me down.

PAUL. Half an hour . . . kick off.

JAN. Give him another five minutes and then . . . if — he was delayed or . . . have a look see what prices they're touting for.

PAUL. Right.

LOUIS. Listen to that . . .

The crowd is singing:
'Que sera, sera,
Whatever will be, will be.
We're going to Wem-ber-ley.
Que sera, sera.'

Makes me feel —

Pause.

I like that. You know, this year Paul —

Pause.

PAUL. What?

LOUIS. I sure glad I'm with you . . . places I seen this year. I ain't done nothing before this year. Best thing that ever happened was going to the factory, meeting you.

PAUL. O.

LOUIS. I'd have just stayed a Millwall supporter, same as everyone else around home, if I ain't met you.

PAUL. You could never have stayed a Millwall supporter Louis. Spiritually, you're The Red Devils.

LOUIS. O Christ, yeah. But —

Pause.

Hard to feel it, you know. Without me proper gear. [Wish me mum hadn't hidden them. See, she thought there was going to be a lot of aggro.

PAUL. It's the cup final for Christ's sake. Anyway, that's all paper talk. Bloody papers.

JAN. Paper's full of it for that Cardiff match. That's what started it. 'Streets of fear,' they said. And all these Welshmen barricading their windows and closing pubs and setting dogs on us. Then they blame us for protecting ourselves. Papers make us sound like animals.

Pause.]

LOUIS. That singing . . . like church.

JAN. Church?

LOUIS. I . . . me mum and dad used to make us all go to church. Didn't you never go to church?

JAN *and* PAUL *look at each other.*

Singing makes me think of church, choir and that.

PAUL. You've found a new religion now.

LOUIS. Right. Got to have faith in something.

PAUL. The Reds!

LOUIS. I just wished . . . weren't so far to go every other week.

JAN. If they had any gumption they'd move to London. If Manchester United played all their home matches in London, capital city — they'd have 200,000 a week turn out. On average. Everyone'd flock to them. Arsenal'd get no-one.

PAUL. Leave off you daft prick. The whole point of Manchester United being in Manchester is — you stupid prat.

JAN. I just meant.

LOUIS. It'd save a packet if they were.

PAUL. No better thing to spend money on.

LOUIS. No. No, no better thing.

Pause. They listen to the singing.

JAN. At least we're here, on the day.

PAUL. Oh, we're here. And we're going to see the match.

JAN. Uncle Harold won't let me down.

LOUIS. Such a beautiful day for it.

JAN. All weathers, the team that wins the cup.

LOUIS. What?

JAN. The team that wins the cup — all weathers.

PAUL. What's he going on about?

JAN. I mean, the team that wins the cup — they've got to be able to play in all weathers.

PAUL. O yeah, definitely.

Silence.

JAN. All weathers, the team that wins the cup.

PAUL. Definitely. Hey —

JAN. What?

PAUL. Look . . . coming up there —

JAN. Christ, the top hat . . . looks like him . . . well, can't see him, but looks like his top hat. See I told you, he wouldn't let me down . . . that's me Uncle Harold for you.

PAUL. You sure it's him . . .

JAN. Wait till he gets past that row of coaches . . . see, I'm like a son to him, his favoured son, he says. After me dad pissed off, me Uncle Harold come round one night, he was really great to me . . . had this bike he give me . . . said to me mum, 'I shall treat Jan like me own favoured son.' I told you he wouldn't let me down, that's him, that's him all right. I won't be a tick . . . this is it boys —

LOUIS. Fantastic!

PAUL. Bloody great.

JAN. We're in . . . won't be a tick . . .

PAUL. Get a move on then . . . wanna see the teams coming out.

JAN. Right. (*He dashes off.*)

LOUIS. Relief.

PAUL. Nar, see Louis son, I told you you'd be all right with me. I told you.

LOUIS. Yeah. This morning, you know —

PAUL. You shouldn't have gone in this morning, you know Louis.

LOUIS. The overtime —

PAUL. O sure, the overtime. But not cup final morning.

LOUIS. When I said I'd do it, I didn't think that it was cup final morning. They all thought I wouldn't get in —

PAUL. Jealousy.

LOUIS. Eh?

PAUL. They're jealous. Bloody jealous. See Louis, before I went there, they hadn't had a real Manchester United fan at the Self Opening Tin Box factory.

LOUIS. Yeah?

PAUL. I was unique. They talked about me . . . I could hear them. Above the noise of the machines, I was on the tin-cutting machine then. The din! But I could hear them . . . see 'em pointing me out . . .'cause I was unique.

LOUIS. I'm unique and all now.

PAUL. No-one else in the spray shop been where you've been this year, seen what you've seen. How many in the spray shop have been to . . . Carlisle, Peterborough, Newcastle and Manchester twenty-four times this year?

Pause.

LOUIS. None. They all get me to talk about it . . . to talk about it you know. Specially old Lil. I miss her.

PAUL. She weren't such a bad lady. Size of her.

LOUIS. Must have been all of sixteen stone. Hey, did she —

PAUL. What?

LOUIS. Don't matter.

PAUL. Go on, what?

LOUIS. I'm not saying nothing against her like.

PAUL. Don't matter if you are. She's left.

[LOUIS. That was great. She always used to say, 'If I win the big prize on the bingo, the golden four thousand, you know what I'd do? I tell you what I'd do: I'll go right up to Reginald Baker and say: "You know what, Regional Baker? You're a big cunt but it ain't as sweet as mine".' (*He laughs.*) And when she won the golden four thousand, she did!

PAUL. Yeah, and I remember what Mr Baker did afterwards. No knocking off five minutes before . . . for a wash and brush up . . . bastard sped up the conveyor belt . . . so at first you didn't notice. There was thirteen thousand cans coming through an hour . . . gallon paint cans and all . . . I'm surprised he ain't got the Queen's Award for Industry yet.]

LOUIS. Paul. Did she grope you?

PAUL. Eh?

LOUIS. Ol' Lil . . . did she finger you?

PAUL. How do you mean? Exactly?

LOUIS. When everyone went to the canal bank dinnertime . . . and she switched off the lights in the spray shop . . . did she used to put her hand down your trousers . . . an' feel you?

Pause.

PAUL. Is that what she did to you?

LOUIS. I thought she did it to everyone.

PAUL. Jan and his Uncle Harold are taking their bloody time.

LOUIS. I can't see them.

PAUL. How often did she do that?

LOUIS. What?

PAUL. Old Lil.

LOUIS. I don't wanna talk about it . . . she was disgusting.

PAUL. I didn't know about that.

LOUIS. The other boys told me — she did it to everyone who worked in the paint shop. Christ, it was hot in there this morning — under the glass roof, heat of the drying ovens . . .

PAUL. Did the other women know?

LOUIS. Eh?

PAUL. The other bints in the spray shop — Hair Lacquer, and Flossie, and that red-haired one with the rubber gloves.

LOUIS. Well, that was the point.

PAUL. What was the point?

LOUIS. At first, in the dark see . . . see, it was really hot, last summer when I started in there . . . and I sat down on the rags in the corner, for a kip, you know. And I must have dropped off . . . and when I woke up, there was old Lil next to me. She was breathing like an old chimney, you know . . . with her big hands down me pants . . . she was really sweating . . . trying to push her tits in me face and that . . . Christ, I laughed.

PAUL. Laughed?

LOUIS. She was laughing and all. And then I saw the other bints . . . they was laughing . . .

Pause.

I'm glad she's left.

PAUL. Right. Come on Jan, for Christ's sake, get a move on.

LOUIS. She weren't a bad lady.

PAUL. I wonder why she never done it to me?

LOUIS. She only does it to the young kids.

Pause.

PAUL. That's what the factory does for you . . . makes everyone look old and washed out.

LOUIS *laughs.*

PAUL. I tell you something Lou boy, they wouldn't fucking try it nowadays . . . see us coming with our Red Devil gear . . . right . . . like the factory . . . no-one tries nothing . . . see it, don't you . . . in their eyes — fear.

LOUIS. Envy.

PAUL. Terror.

LOUIS. I was no-one till . . . someone now.

PAUL. You don't need the bloody Army, Louis — you're in the best bloody Army there is . . . ten minutes, in there — whole legions of us . . . Doc's Red Army . . . our drills and Dr Martins and bob hats . . . union jacks and tartan and no shirts, whatever the weather . . . Christ they envy that . . . singing . . .chanting . . . fever starting and they'll be out . . . jogging, dead nonchalant . . . out into the arena out of the dark and into the sun . . . like bleeding gladiators . . .

The crowd noises off swell, increase in volume.

Doc in front . . . in his best suit . . . rolling the Wrigleys in his mouth . . . Martin Buchan behind . . . on his toes, knees bobbling . . .

LOUIS. Buchan and Forsythy — they're all Scottish, Christ I wish I was Scottish . . .

PAUL. Brian Greenhoff, he ain't Scottish — Hilly, bleeding Cockney —

LOUIS. Christ, Hilly — fucking ace. Pearson . . . dynamite both feet . . . and Stepney. Cockney an' all.

PAUL. Houston — Coppell . . . Dally . . . McCreery . . . McIlroy and . . .

LOUIS. Lou himself.

PAUL. Gotta be there, gotta be there —

Great roars.

Enter JAN *in tears.*

PAUL. Jan —

LOUIS. Hey, what's up?

JAN. I . . . I . . .

PAUL. That was yer Uncle Harold —

JAN. Yeah —

PAUL. Well, you got them?

JAN *hesitates.*

JAN. See, the bloke with him was the bloke who —

PAUL. Didn't he have the tickets then?

JAN. He had them but, what I'm saying is: the bloke with him was the bloke who let him have the carpets cost price. And he's asked the bloke who services his carpet showroom vans cost price.

PAUL. Shit.

JAN. And the garage bloke brought his son.

PAUL. Fuck.

JAN. And the bloke down his road who put in a bathroom suite cost price.

PAUL. O . . . O great.

JAN. Me Uncle Harold was really sick about it.

PAUL. Yeah?

JAN. He said, Jan — I feel as if I've let you down.

PAUL *and* LOUIS *exchange looks.*

PAUL. Very sensitive bloke your Uncle Harold.

JAN. Oh, he is. He knew how sick I felt. See, he'd done his bit, he'd got a ticket for himself and another three.

PAUL. Hat-trick.

JAN. He said the carpet bloke had talked him into it. In the Albion last night. He said if the carpet bloke hadn't bought him six double scotches . . . he said he knew he was being conned. So he went to the bog for a piss, to think how to get out of it, and he pissed over the garage bloke's Hush Puppies. So he give him a ticket as a way of apologising.

PAUL. If he'd thrown up, I suppose he'd have given him a handful?

LOUIS. But how could he do it, Jan? I mean — how? He'd promised them to us —

JAN. He said, he'd use his best endeavours.

LOUIS. What?

JAN. I mean, be fair — that's . . . O Christ.

Pause. JAN really cries.

Let you down . . . I let you down . . . sorry.

Pause.

LOUIS. Weren't your fault, Jan.

JAN. He promised me.

PAUL. If I see him.

Pause.

He better not let me see him. I'll fucking . . .
Jesus, I'll open his face with a fucking
bottle.
Take out his eyes with a corkscrew.
Ground a bottle in his face till it's freckled
with splinters of broken glass.
He'll be a fucking red devil all right.
All blood! (*He stands breathing heavily.*)
Behind that wall — (*He shrieks.*) Behind that
wall. If it weren't for that wall. (*He
runs at the wall; smashes himself into it.*)

JAN. Sorry Paul.

Silence. PAUL looks for something to smash.

PAUL. Still time, find a tout . . . get a ticket, there must be hundreds. All them celebrities that get the free ones, they unload them on the touts. No problem, we'll have tickets all right. We'll be in there. Might miss the teams coming out. But we'll be in there, all right. No trouble.

Pause.

Leave it to me. I'll shoot down there . . . Lou, you look for a tranny — bloke on the hot-dog stall over there had a tranny — get the tranny, while he ain't looking. Nick his tranny.

LOUIS. Could have watched it on telly at home — not stand here listening to it on a tranny —

PAUL. Take the tranny inside. Watching the match and then we can listen to the interviews with the players afterwards. Right?

JAN. Yeah . . .

PAUL. You Jan, son. You can get some hot-dogs to nosh. Some cokes and all. Distract the bloke while Lou fingers the tranny, right?

JAN. Right!

PAUL. Gonna be all right, in't it.

JAN. They was only standing seats.

LOUIS. Tickets — standing tickets.

JAN. Uncle Harold was choked about that. He said he'd expected seats. He said we'd be better off with seats anyway.

PAUL. I'll get seats then.

JAN. Right.

PAUL. Your bread —

JAN. Go up to . . . twenty quid.

LOUIS. Twenty?

PAUL. You got twenty?

LOUIS. Well . . . okay.

PAUL. What better thing to spend money on anyway?

A crescendo of roars off.
The band starts to play 'Abide With Me'.

JAN. O Jesus . . . they've brought it back.

PAUL. 'Abide With Me'.

JAN. They stopped it at the Cup Final. I thought they stopped it at the Cup Final.

PAUL. They brought it back . . . for United. Wembley anthem.

LOUIS. It's a hymn.

PAUL. If the band hadn't played this hymn, Doc's Red Army would have fucking killed 'em.

JAN. Makes me go cold.

LOUIS. They . . . sung this at church a lot . . . when I used to go. I didn't know it was part of the Cup Final. Didn't know then. Always liked it. I asked the preacher once, I said, 'What's it mean?'

PAUL. Mean?

LOUIS. 'Abide with me,' he says. 'It means — like, tolerate. Means tolerate me. Like if you do a lot of things wrong, there must be a reason, so He . . . tolerates you.'

PAUL. Stuff all that. It means — Wembley, the Cup Final. United in that tunnel, banging their studs on the cement . . . smelling of liniment and shirts brand new, smelling brand new . . . and waiting, ready to go out into the sun. We'll be there, get these tickets and —

He hesitates.

The singing of 'Abide With Me' is very loud. JAN, *then* LOUIS, *and finally PAUL join in the singing, standing holding their arms up, scarves stretched between their hands. They sway in time to the music. The hymn swells.*

The lights dim to fade. The music continues louder.

Scene Two

The same, later.
Roaring crowd behind the wall.
JAN *sits on a rubbish bin, listening to a transistor radio.*
LOUIS *paces, eating a hot-dog, sipping a coke.*

JAN. We're all over them. We're murdering them. It's going to be a rout. Hang on — (*He listens to the radio.*) Fucking hell, that was Hilly! Turner blocked it with his feet. Bloody feet. Oh yeah, we're murdering them. Great, fantastic.

LOUIS (*no enthusiasm*). Yeah.

Pause.

Paul's taking his time.

JAN. Yeah, didn't think . . . didn't think it'd take this long.

LOUIS. Jan . . .

Pause.

JAN. What?

LOUIS. We're going to get in, aren't we.

Pause.

JAN. Paul'll sort it out. Paul's magic, for sorting out stuff. We never had tickets for Hillsborough. Paul sorted it out.

LOUIS. Different at Hillsborough. There was more tickets. Clubs get a better allocation for the semi-final. It's bloody lousy, way it is for the final. [Why don't they give enough for all the true fans.

JAN. Well, see, like me Uncle Harold explained it. It's an occasion. A national asset the Cup Final. That's why it's not just the finalists' fans who get in. That's why they give a third of the tickets to dignitaries. He said.

LOUIS. Dignitaries?

JAN. Well, see. Like . . . celebrities, who make society tick.

LOUIS. Eh?

JAN. I dunno, I didn't understand it.]

LOUIS. Sixty thousand week in week out at United. What about the Irish fans?

JAN. Christ, yeah.

LOUIS. Every week from Dublin, they said. Twenty-seven quid it costs them, to every home match. Great blokes. Great blokes.

JAN. Yeah, I really like it when we're on the same train as them.

LOUIS. None of them had tickets for the final.

JAN. No, well — they're Irish.

LOUIS. They spend twenty-seven quid for every home match. They don't earn much. All their money for United, and then they don't get to see the final.

JAN. Well, the dignitaries —

LOUIS. What fucking dignitaries?

Silence.

JAN. Well like — this is how me Uncle Harold explained it. Like see, the Arabs. They wanted to see the Cup Final.

LOUIS. I want to see the cup final.

JAN. Well like, now they've got all this dough. Like, if they want to buy a fleet of warships or something, to smooth 'em up, so they buy British ones, like — what happens is, the Ministry of Defence gets onto the FA, like and says, 'Give us twenty tickets.'

LOUIS. Yeah.

JAN. Then they buy the warships.

LOUIS. Right.

Pause.

All them women though — they ain't buying warships.

JAN. Wives and that. Bints who knock about with dignitaries.

LOUIS. Bint on TV last night — she didn't even know both teams had the same colours.

JAN. No, she didn't.

Pause.

Pearson's having a brilliant game according to this —

LOUIS. 'Ark at them. O Christ. How high do you reckon that wall is.

JAN. I dunno.

LOUIS. Maybe we could get over it.

JAN. Glass at the top.

LOUIS. Yeah, but . . . what's a bit of glass — to see United in the final?

Pause.

Yeah well. There's hardly anyone down there now.

They look.

[JAN. Me grandad hated football.

LOUIS. What?

JAN. Just thinking. Ol' grandpa, he hated football he did. Said he stopped watching it after the war. Said, 'All them years of war fighting the Germans, then we play them at football.' 'Football's better than war,' I says. 'Yeah,' he says. 'They should have thought of that before they started the war.']

LOUIS. It'd been fairer if there was a queue, you know, you could queue for tickets.

JAN. Yeah.

LOUIS. Starting, say, right after the semis. You queue up. First come, first served.

JAN. I'd have queued for days.

LOUIS. Weeks.

JAN. I'd have taken me holidays to queue.

LOUIS. Right.

The crowd roars.

LOUIS. What was that?

JAN. Turner just got in the way of Daly — let fly. What a boy! We're all over them, the country bumpkins don't know what day it is. Eh, what's that? Bloke here reckons McCalliog's playing . . . not bad.

LOUIS. McCalliog. He can't play.

JAN. Course he can't play. Stands to reason, that Doc wouldn't have let him go if he could play. The Doc saw him, thought — Christ, what a wanker, you can go. He can't play.

LOUIS. No.

JAN. Bloke here don't know what he's talking about. Says he's playing all right. Shows bloke here don't know nothing.

LOUIS. If I was the Bionic Man —

JAN. If I was the Bionic Man, I could see through that bloody wall.

LOUIS. That's what I mean.

JAN. Or leap over it.

LOUIS. Right.

Pause. LOUIS *mimes the Bionic Man.*

JAN. Tell me, Bionic Man — what can you see?

LOUIS. Oh, it is great, son. It is fantastic. I wish you could see what I can see. The colours . . . the movement. Darting about . . . in their blood red shirts — shorts so white . . . Southampton in gold and blue . . . pitch as green as a rubber plant and the crowd swaying with their flags . . . The ball's orange . . . looks like a billiard table. It's great.

JAN. All I can see is a wall . . .

LOUIS. You ain't the Bionic Man . . . *Just see James Dean standing outside Wembley — if he wanted to get in.

JAN. Eh?

LOUIS. Old Jimmy, he'd just crash through the wall, he would. Nick a motor, and smash through the gates.*

Another roar.

LOUIS. What was that?

JAN. Oh, that was Southampton — miles wide and over.

LOUIS. Stepney had it covered.

JAN. Yeah.

LOUIS. Did he say that?

JAN. Goes without saying.

LOUIS. Osgood can't shoot, not from thirty yards and no-one'll let him get closer than that.

JAN. It weren't Osgood. It was McCalliog.

LOUIS. No danger.

JAN. No.

LOUIS. I mean, if McCalliog was the sort of bloke who ever looked like scoring, the Doc wouldn't have let him go.

JAN. Right.

Pause.

LOUIS. If I had a length of rope and an anchor, we'd be in.

Pause.

A length of plastic-coated, grade three rope and a metal hook with a claw, we'd be in.

JAN. How?

LOUIS. Commando training. Commando training mate. Oh, a wall like that. Show a wall like that to a commando and he'd piss himself.

JAN. Yeah?

LOUIS. Even a green recruit with just three weeks' basic training, show him a wall like that and he'd piss himself, he'd say: 'You must be joking mate.' With just three weeks' basic training, plus the equipment — the plastic-coated, grade three rope and half a dozen anchors — you'd get five hundred commandoes over that wall and inside in three minutes.

Pause.

JAN. Pity we ain't got no rope or anchors.

LOUIS. Yeah.

JAN. Is that what you tried to sign up for?

LOUIS. What?

JAN. A commando?

LOUIS. Oh, not a commando, no. I wouldn't mind being a
commando, but I didn't try that. I mean, they only take the
cream, just the cream. I thought: well, I know I ain't the
cream. You've got to be the cream. I didn't think it was
worth trying the commandoes, since I didn't have a chance.
I thought I'd try something where I had a chance, you know.
Avoid the frustration of getting turned down.

JAN. Yeah.

LOUIS. So I tried what I thought I had a chance, a good chance.
That's what bugged me, getting turned down.

JAN. It would.

The crowd roars.

JAN. Hilly, header — over.

LOUIS. We're murdering them.

JAN. Yeah. There was a mate of mine who went to Paris. And he
got really pissed, so pissed. On that aniseed drink. Makes you
really pissed, so next morning, if you drink a glass of water
you get pissed all over again.

LOUIS. Commandoes ain't allowed to touch that stuff. Not
allowed to drink, except after a mission successfully
accomplished.

JAN. Well, he was in the navy, see.

LOUIS. Rum.

JAN. And he ended up in Paris with a few blokes and got
smashed out of his head on this aniseed drink. An', he signed
up for the foreign legion. Walked in pissed and said, 'I want
to sign up.' So they give him the form and he signed up.
For thirty years. And when he sobered up he was in the
Sahara.

LOUIS. Christ.

JAN. Only another twenty-seven years and he's out.

LOUIS. Jesus.

JAN. His mum was arf annoyed.

LOUIS. I wish me mum ain't hidden me Dr Martins.

JAN. His mum said to my mum, she said, 'Tony he's always
been difficult, always had problems with him. But this time
he's gone too far.'

LOUIS. I wouldn't mind joining the foreign legion. To forget.

JAN. Yeah.

LOUIS. If I had wanted to forget, I'd sign up like a shot.

JAN. He'll be an old man when he comes out.

LOUIS. There's some vicious bastards in the foreign legion. Vicious.

JAN. He don't send nothing home neither. At least when he was in the navy he sent something home.

LOUIS. They've been playing fifteen minutes.

JAN. Yeah.

LOUIS. Paul'll go spare if we don't get in.

JAN. It ain't my fault.

LOUIS. I'm not saying it's your fault. Put it this way: I wouldn't like to be in your Uncle Harold's shoes if Paul sees him.

JAN. No.

LOUIS. He shouldn't have done that, Jan. Shouldn't have promised.

JAN. How do you think I feel.

Silence. The crowd is gently murmuring off.

Enter PAUL. He looks livid. He paces, turns, grimaces, smashes his fist against the wall.

No luck?

PAUL glares at him.

PAUL. Fucking tout — asking, asking twenty-five quid for a standing ticket. Twenty-five quid for one. Jesus.

Pause.

LOUIS. Bit steep.

PAUL. Held it up, he did. In his hand, held it up. Said, 'How much am I offered?' Great crowd round him. Blokes in suits, ties and that. Posh voice, said 'Thirty quid.' He got it. Cunt. Flash cunt. (*He paces about again.*)

JAN. We . . . ain't gonna get in, are we?

Pause.

LOUIS. I was saying, if only I had a thirty foot length of rope and an anchor — over the top.

PAUL. Is that all you need? What have I got here? (*He pats his pockets.*) Electric toothbrush, complete works of Charles Dickens, packet of three, six light bulbs and a set of sparking plugs but . . . no anchor and no thirty foot length of rope. Sorry.

Pause.

This is disgusting. Disgusting. This shouldn't be allowed. Shouldn't be allowed. Twenty odd times I've been to Manchester this year. An' to Wolverhampton, Burnley, Sheffield. To Birmingham, Ipswich, Villa Park, Newcastle, Liverpool, Middlesbrough, Derby. An' Leicester and Stoke and Leeds and Coventry. All that, on fares. Standing in the train, five hours . . . eight hours . . . standing up in wet clothes, no fucking food on the train . . . standing up in the rain on the terraces . . . like . . . cattle. No roof to keep the rain off . . . Lavatories stinking like cess-pits. Warm beer in paper cups . . . no food at the grounds . . . herded about by the cops. No wonder they call us animals. That's how they fucking treat us. (*He growls, impersonating an ape.*)

JAN *and* LOUIS *laugh, goad him on. He behaves more ape. He stops.*

They treat dogs better. That's 'cause we're fucking animals, Lou, son.

LOUIS (*acts ape*). Yeah.

PAUL. Treat people like animals, that's how they act. Those bloody lavatories at most of the football grounds in England — if they were like that at the factory Lou, everyone'd walk out. Strike until they're cleaned up. Bloody clubs expect you to pay to get into them.

LOUIS. I reckon I missed about fifteen goals this season, 'cause I couldn't see.

PAUL. Whole day and twenty quid to see the match at Coventry and I couldn't see either fucking goal. Talked to this bloke who went to Holland one year . . . see United against Ajax. Oh, it's a different world over there. Never have to bother over there . . . sit down . . . bring round beer and lovely hot food, waiters do . . . while you're sitting there, while the match is on . . . like a fucking night club, not like a football ground . . . all the geezers take their bints . . . great.

LOUIS. Like cricket.

PAUL. Eh?

LOUIS. Never have no riots at cricket.

PAUL. Well, not often.

JAN. Never have no aggro at Wimbledon — tennis and that.

LOUIS. Treat you better. You can see. Get something for your money more than the game.

JAN. Don't exploit you.

PAUL. You what?

JAN. Me Uncle . . . Tom —

PAUL. Oh.

JAN. Said he hates being exploited. His governor exploited him he said. He told him what to do. Where to go.

PAUL. I wish . . .

Pause.

There was something else. To make me blood bubble, to look forward to . . . to . . . mean something.

Pause.

There was this boy I used to know . . . a student, at the factory, one summer . . . for a bit of pocket money, he worked a couple of weeks . . . then Mr Baker found out about him and got him out of the factory so fast you couldn't see him move. Junkie, see. O yeah. I saw him after, in the High Street. Said it happened at the Black Lion. Lot of pushers there. An' he didn't want to know. They pumped him with the stuff. Held him down and shot it into him . . . and then, later, after he'd got hooked, they wouldn't always sell him it, 'cause they kept putting up the price. See. An' he said, 'Cunts, they got me hooked an' then said no.' (*He paces, turns.*) Bloody football clubs. Get you hooked, get you boiling, get the fever rushing through you — all of them, build it up, get a head of steam and then when it explodes, wash their hands of you, call you animals, say piss off we don't want you. (*Pause.*) An' they know they've got you hooked. That you can't do without them. That seems more of a crime to me. Than the crimes we're supposed to do.

LOUIS. At least we'll be able to see it on the telly tomorrer.

PAUL. Fucking Jesus.

LOUIS. That's blasphemy.

PAUL. So what. God's dead. They killed him in the war.

LOUIS. No.

PAUL. Up there, laid out his corpse and wrapped it in a sky blue shroud. Shows he was always a fucking Manchester City supporter.

More roars off.

Christ, what's happening. Jan, what's —

LOUIS. A goal! We've scored! We're winning —

PAUL. Nar, weren't loud enough for a goal. Jan, the radio.

JAN (*struggling with it*). Bloody dial — busted.

PAUL. What — give's.

JAN. Bloody dial fucked, or the batteries gone flat.

LOUIS. What happened? Gotta know what happened —

JAN. I can't help it —

PAUL. Pissing hell.

LOUIS. It must be a goal, it must be a goal!

JAN. Sod it.

LOUIS. We're winning — we must be winning —

PAUL. Get that radio —

JAN. I can't Paul, it's smashed.

PAUL. Smashed, I'll fucking smash it — (*He hurls the radio against the wall. The plastic casing smashes, the radio falls to the floor in pieces.* PAUL *stands breathing raggedly.*)

JAN. You've busted it . . . we'll never find out who scored now.

LOUIS. I wanted to see that . . . wanted to see that.

PAUL *lets out an animal cry and runs against the wall, smashing himself against it.*

LOUIS. Paul, for Christ's sake.

PAUL. If it weren't for that wall.

LOUIS. Paul, don't be a stoopid bastard, you'll —

PAUL. There's always a fucking wall in the way. Always get so far, and there's a wall to block it. Smash it down, smash it down —

He charges it again. LOUIS *tries to stop him.*
PAUL hits the wall and screams. He crumples to the floor.
A great roar from the crowd.
JAN and LOUIS approach the wall. PAUL *lies there groaning.*

JAN. Better find the St John's men.

LOUIS. He's mad, he's crazy.

JAN. Yeah.

LOUIS. I wonder who scored?

The roars grow, the lights fade.

Blackout.

Scene Three

Later. The sound of the crowd roaring.
Lights up.
LOUIS *is fixing the radio with a plastic spoon.*
The roars continue.
Enter JAN.

JAN. Still nil-nil.

LOUIS. Oh.

JAN. Apparently it's all United. Southampton are right
   knackered. They're soaking up so much punishment. The
   bloke on the ice-cream van said — he's got a portable telly.

LOUIS. See it?

JAN. Nar, there was such a crowd there. Anyway he said it looks
   like there'll be an avalanche in the last twenty minutes. Six
   or seven goals.

LOUIS. Great.

JAN. What you doing?

LOUIS. Fixing the tranny.

JAN (*looks*). Bloody hell. You've . . . got it all back together.

LOUIS. Yeah, still ain't working yet, but —

JAN. I didn't know you could fix radios.

LOUIS. Me sister's husband, he does radios an' that. In the navy.
   Wireless operator. Real skill. He'll make a bomb when he gets

out. Electronics an' that. Tried to get me to have a go at it.
I said, 'Leave off: I work in a factory mate. No chance.' So's
he tried to show me how to do it. An' showed me how
trannys work.

JAN. Christ. I didn't know you was good at that sort of thing.

LOUIS. No? *Learned the basics on me refrigeration course.*

The crowd roars.

JAN. It'll be good to hear the last fifteen minutes.

LOUIS. If I can get it fixed . . . see, it's the . . . I dunno how to
explain it, I dunno what the things are called.

JAN. Well, so long as you can fix it — that's the important thing.

LOUIS. Is it?

JAN. Sure, course it is. That's what counts.

LOUIS. Pity the recruiting officer didn't agree.

JAN. Oh.

LOUIS. Told him I could fix radios. An' phones. An' alarm
clocks. He said there's not much call for alarm clock repairs
in Belfast.

Pause.

He was right sarcastic. The other bloke weren't so bad. He
said: 'Look son, you ain't got too much going for you at the
moment. But if you can prove yourself as a competent
electrician, if you learn a bit more, come back in a year and
we'll have another look at you.'

JAN. Oh.

LOUIS. At two o'clock in the afternoon.

JAN. Eh?

LOUIS. I wrote it down when to go back. I'll go back then. Me
brother-in-law, when he's on leave, he's going to show me a
few things. Get me to look a bit competent as an electrician,
and then, well — fingers crossed, I'm keeping me fingers crossed.

JAN. Bit difficult mending wirelesses with crossed fingers, in't
it?

They laugh.

LOUIS. Come in handy on the Plain though —

JAN. Eh?

LOUIS. With the cadets, two weeks, Salisbury. Full manoeuvres. Had to do everything, we did. Guard duty, rifle range, camping, oh a lot of camping. Food never tastes so good as when you're out in the open . . .

JAN. I remember when you come back — so energetic!

LOUIS. It's a different world. Just like the Army, it is. Like a family. Looks after you, looks after you.

Pause.

JAN. More bloody reliable than me Uncle Harold.

LOUIS. Well —

JAN. When me dad pissed off, he said he'd treat me like his own son.

Pause.

His son never hears from him neither.

Pause.

Me grandad always said they'd hang Harold.

LOUIS. They don't hang people no more.

JAN. Me grandad said they'd bring back hanging specially for him.

LOUIS. You oughta join the cadets, Jan. That's what you oughta do.

JAN. I want to . . . be part of something.

LOUIS. Yeah —

JAN. Like when we're standing there . . . on the Stretford End . . . crushed in, thousands of us . . . and 'cause you're in the red and white, it don't matter that no-one knows you, 'cause you're like brothers, so close . . . all together . . . all together . . . and all leaning together, the same way, and all breathing together, like, not thousands of people, but like one . . . like a great giant breathing . . .

The crowd's roars subside.

I wish it could be like that every day of the week. Better than the fucking factory.

LOUIS. Give it a try on Thursday . . . that way, get in, enlist, it'll be like it all the time, every day of the week.

JAN. Well?

LOUIS. Thursday night.

JAN. I'll have . . . a look. But I ain't saying I'll join.

LOUIS. Thursday then.

JAN. Right.

Enter PAUL, *his head bandaged.*

PAUL. Would have to be the same fucking eye.

JAN. Paul — you all right?

PAUL. Yeah, I'm all right. Couple of stitches.

JAN. Oh —

PAUL. No anaesthetic.

LOUIS. No?

PAUL. St John's bloke said, 'I'll give you a shot.' I said, 'Stuff that son, I don't want none of that. Just bung the stitches in.' Still nil-nil.

LOUIS. Yeah.

PAUL. Last ten minutes, there'll be a flood of goals. Two a minute, I reckon. What you doing?

LOUIS. Fixing the tranny. Nearly fixed it.

Silence.

PAUL. Didn't know you could —

LOUIS. Yeah.

PAUL. Oh. You don't want to let Mr Baker hear you can fix radios. An' that. Oh, he'll have you doing all the sodding plug fixing and that, if he knows you can twiddle with wires.

LOUIS. I wouldn't mind that. Out of the spray shop, more money doing electrics than shoving cans through an oven.

Pause.

PAUL. I'd not let Mr Baker hear about that, if I was you. Right Jan?

Pause.

PAUL. I said —

JAN. Right.

Pause.

JAN. At least . . . we was here on the day.

Pause.

Something to tell our grandchildren

PAUL. What?

JAN. Here on the day . . . Man United, the Red Devils, Doc's
Army won the cup . . .

PAUL. Doc's Red Army, an' Doc's cockney army — we'll be
marching tonight, mate . . . oh Christ . . . missed the match,
but — tonight . . . marching through Piccadilly, thousands
of us . . . see the lights going off in the pubs as we approach . . .
be some glass flying tonight, be some glass smashed tonight . . .
worse than the blitz. All together, marching through
London . . .

Pause.

Just the thought of it . . . makes me wanna wet meself.

JAN. Eh?

PAUL. Felt like that after the semi . . . felt it throbbing through
me . . . We'll be marching tonight. Better not catch sight of
your Uncle Harold.

JAN. N-no.

PAUL. Altogether.

JAN. Yeah.

PAUL. No worries, no cares, nothing to have to think about. All
that obliterated, just the —

LOUIS. Like the cadets, Jan.

PAUL. Eh?

LOUIS. Plunge in, no cares, altogether.

PAUL. Wrong army.

LOUIS. No.

Long pause.

PAUL. You fixed that radio yet?

LOUIS. Almost.

PAUL. Gonna be a replay . . .

JAN. Still ten minutes.

PAUL. They'll close the game up now . . . too much to risk losing.
Here again, Thursday night. We'll fucking have tickets then.

LOUIS. I thought it was Wednesday —

PAUL. Thursday.

LOUIS. But Thursday, see Thursday —

Pause.

PAUL. What?

LOUIS. Thursday, well, every Thursday, cadets' night.

Pause.

Go on Thursdays to the cadets.

PAUL. Not when United are playing.

LOUIS. They never play on a Thursday.

PAUL. This Thursday, the replay —

LOUIS. But Paul . . . got to have a hundred per cent record. For the regular army, got to prove I'm hundred per cent.

PAUL. Lou baby, you've gotta get your priorities right, son.

LOUIS. I seen all the matches.

PAUL. Can't miss the replay. Can he Jan?

Silence. The crowd is roaring.

LOUIS. But Paul.

PAUL. Can't let everyone down Lou.

LOUIS. Won't make no difference whether I'm there or not.

PAUL (*grabs him*). Lou, kiddo — United need you.

LOUIS. Need me? They don't need me. Or you. Or Jan. Don't give a fuck about us. How come we're outside if they need us? Cadets need me, make me a part of them, take me in, give me food, give me a home, give me . . . a job. Give me something to do. United don't give a shit. Take me money, that's all.

PAUL. No . . . they've got us all, got you . . . you can't do without them.

LOUIS. Gonna try hard Paul.

PAUL. Tell him Jan.

Silence. Roars.

PAUL. Jan, I said —

JAN. Gotta come Lou. Gotta come.

LOUIS. Want the army, Paul. Like you want it Jan.

PAUL. Jan, don't be a prick — Jan don't want —

LOUIS. Be someone?

PAUL. Is someone. Right Jan? Down your road, when you set out in your drills and tartan, eh?

LOUIS. When I set out in my cadets drills and —

PAUL. Lou, son —

   [*They struggle.*

   You're fucking coming.

LOUIS. Ain't throwing it away, boy. Ain't gonna be like you when I'm your age. Factory six days, life on one? That ain't a life. That ain't living.

   LOUIS *pulls away.*
   PAUL *flicks a knife, holds it towards* LOUIS.

   Aw don't be stupid. I'm on your side.

PAUL. You've changed sides.

JAN. Paul . . . he's Lou.

PAUL. Done things for you Lou, son, done things for you this year. At Sheffield when they got you in the bog, twenty of them . . . when you went in the wrong bog and they got you, I waded in . . . kicked his fucking head in to release you.

LOUIS. You didn't do that for me, Paul. You did it cause you get your fix kicking fucking heads in. Me, I was just the excuse.

PAUL. Did it for you . . . 'cause you're one of Doc's soldiers.

LOUIS. No Paul . . . put it away Paul . . .

JAN. Not today, Paul . . . not on the cup final. No sense of occasion.

PAUL. You sound like your fucking Uncle Harold. Cunt —

JAN. Good bloke.

PAUL. What's he ever done for you?

JAN. Visited me in the home every week, some boys had no-one visit them.

PAUL. Bollocks. He was probably screwing the matron.

JAN. Paul . . . drop it, let it drop.

PAUL. You're gonna be here Thursday Lou, gonna be here at the replay.]

LOUIS *begins to shake his head.*
PAUL *goes to lunge at him but the crowd lets our a deafening roar. It continues loud.*

JAN. Christ.

PAUL. That's a goal.

JAN. Scored!

PAUL. Jesus.

JAN. Just before the death —

Euphoria. They leap about. Embrace. LOUIS *stands apart from them. The roars continue.*

PAUL. Musta been Pearson —

JAN. Hill was going close.

PAUL. Radio working Lou — quick.

LOUIS. Working. (*He hands the radio to* PAUL.)

PAUL. Only joking see, no problem. Thursday, cadets all right. No replay now — we've done it . . . oh great. (*He holds the radio to one ear.*)

JAN. Who scored it . . . got the station. Who —

PAUL *is deathly. Pause. The roars continue.*

PAUL. Stokes.

Pause.

JAN. Own goal?

Pause.

PAUL. McCalliog split the defence with a long through-ball and Stokes . . . put it in the corner.

Pause.

JAN. It's not possible.

PAUL. Fucking radio ain't lying.

Pause.

O Jesus. (*He holds his head.*)

JAN. Five minutes to go still . . .

PAUL *looks at him.*

O Christ. (JAN *is almost tearful.*)

PAUL. How's it possible? How's it possible? After all we've done this season . . . so far, so much . . . days in trains, all that attacking, all that . . . fighting . . . pipped for the league and now . . .

LOUIS *edges away.*

Where you sneaking off to?

LOUIS. I'm going home.

PAUL. Match ain't over.

LOUIS. It is now.

PAUL. When the mob gets out . . .tonight, oh tonight there'll be fucking hell break loose.

LOUIS. That's why I'm going home.

Pause.

I'll come round for you Thursday, Jan.

He goes.

PAUL. What's he mean by that?

Pause.

JAN. Dunno. Dunno what he means.

Pause. The roars continue.

PAUL. He's gone. He's chicken. He's a wank. There, that's what happens when ol' Lil gropes you.

JAN. She used to grope everyone.

PAUL. Did she grope you?

JAN. Used to, till Lou came.

PAUL. I wonder why she never groped me.

Pause.

Tonight . . . oh Christ, tonight . . . it'll be like . . . He weren't trying to chat you into joining the fucking army was he?

Pause.

Said —

JAN. The cadets, he made it sound like . . . a family.

PAUL. We're your family. United, the biggest family in the land . . . oh tonight, you'll see tonight . . . it'll be like after

the Spurs match . . . after coming back from White Hart
Lane . . . we'll assemble at Euston . . . we'll march in file,
wave after wave of us . . . the streets'll empty as we
approach . . .

The lights begin to fade.
JAN *goes the way* LOUIS *went.*
PAUL *is alone stage centre.*
*As the lights fade, a spot continues to illuminate his face until
only his face is lit.*

They'll barricade the windows, the pubs'll lock their doors,
the lights will go off in the shops and the police will line the
pavements, white with fear . . . cops' hats'll bobble like
decorations on a windy promenade . . . the air will be heavy
with shouts and yells and the smashing of glass . . . No-one
will ignore us. We will not be ignored. They'll talk about us,
write about us, hate us. Hate us. Hate us. Animals, call us
animals . . . not ignore me . . . won't be ignored . . . not
ignore me . . . not . . . ignore . . . me.

The lights go to black.
More roars.
End of play.

IN THE CITY

The third part of BARBARIANS

In The City received its first production at the Greenwich Theatre, London on 29 September 1977 in the treble bill entitled BARBARIANS, with the following cast:

PAUL   Nick Edmett
JAN   Karl Johnson
LOUIS   Jeffery Kissoon

Directed by Keith Hack
Designed by Voytek

Enter JAN *in soldier's uniform; he speaks to the audience as though the audience were a policeman.*

JAN. What do you mean? I ain't doing nothing wrong. I'm on embarkation leave. Ain't I? Just come for the Carnival. No I ain't on duty. What, here? Leave off. This is London! Soldiers in the streets, you must be joking! I'm not telling you me name. You tell me your name copper. All right, all right . . .

PAUL enters and addresses the audience, reading a copy of Time Out.
He wears dark glasses.

PAUL. 'Attractive intelligent American woman. I'm not tired of London, but only of selfish people only wanting to receive but not to give. Wide cultural interests. Seeks attractive, aware, sensitive bachelor with crazy sense of humour . . .'

PAUL laughs crazily.
He reads on silently.

JAN. See, here's me ID. All right, going tomorrow yeah. Cross the old pond to . . . You know. Just have a good time tonight. Last few hours in London till . . . when I'm back. No, no weapons. Honest. Not when I'm on leave . . . just come for the Carnival . . .

PAUL. 'Sensitive gay guy, North Acton, twenty-eight, non-scener into rock films seeks active guy 21-25 for sincere relationship.' (*He looks at the audience.*) Disgusting, filth, bloody pervert.

JAN. Thanks, very decent of you. Just, where's the Carnival? I mean, is it coming down here soon? Do you know the route?

PAUL approaches JAN.

PAUL. Sieg heil!

JAN. Fucking hot.

PAUL. Will be later.

JAN. Uniform, I meant.

PAUL. Oh, very nice, very smart — very you.

JAN. Feels funny.

PAUL. You make me feel safe, you know.

JAN. What?

PAUL. Standing next to you, I feel all safe and secure.

JAN. You taking the piss?

PAUL. Nar, nar. I mean — I really am thinking, thank Christ I ain't got no Irish blood in me. No doubt about it. England rules, OK.

JAN. Bloody serge though. It makes me leg itch. Especially in this heat. First couple of weeks at Aldershot, it gave me a rash.

PAUL. Diddums.

JAN. It was impetigo. All sores all over me body. They got to me face. They said I looked like a werewolf.

PAUL. Oi!

JAN. It weren't funny. There was a plague of it. In the barracks. Everyone had it who was going to Belfast.

PAUL. O yerr.

JAN. Bloody sarge, he's a right hard nut. Goes for a six mile run every day. He said it was psychosomatic. 'Cause we was going to Belfast. That's what he said. He said we was weak-gutted, goldfish-livered yellow cowards. (*Pause.*) He was a bit cross. 'Cause they had to put the posting back. MO — doctor — said we couldn't contaminate the inhabitants of Belfast. With the plague. Like, the impetigo.

PAUL. Bit of a comedian, is he?

JAN. That's why they put the postings back.

PAUL. How do you feel?

JAN. O well. (*Pause.*) You know, can't believe it's me, going. (*Pause.*) Bloody funny feeling I can tell you. Tomorrow. Embarkation. At 18.00 hours. Into the battlefield. (*Pause.*) I joined up to become a pastry chef.

PAUL. Well, make mince-pies of the Micks.

JAN. Yeah, our lads'll show them. We'll fucking show them.

PAUL. Give you a few memories to take tonight, son. Tonight, give you a few memories all right. Carnival, bints all lined up. Be here.

JAN. That's why I thought I'd wear me drills. You know, really impress them. Me sarge says women go weak at the knees when they see a highly trained soldier.

PAUL. As opposed to a highly trained pastry chef.

JAN. Yeah.

PAUL. You're a man.

JAN. I am.

PAUL. A man. No doubt about it. A bit of a loon, but — a man.

JAN. A loon?

PAUL. Fucking going to Belfast! You must be outa your head. I wouldn't set foot in Kilburn High Street after the pubs've closed. I thought you'd have more sense son. Got out of the posting.

JAN. I signed up for seven years. Ready to go — when Her Majesty called.

PAUL. There was a hundred things you could have done to get out of it. Made out you'd gone berserk, or queer, or kept wetting the bed.

JAN. Wetting the bed?

PAUL. Yeah, like drink twenty pints every night and keep pissing the bed. They would have kicked you out then. Christ, 'course they would have. High risk you'd have been. Might have drowned the whole bloody unit. (*Pause.*) Well, enjoy tonight.

JAN. Yeah. Last night in London till . . . 'Course I'll be back.

PAUL. Right. It's all arranged. Anything you want son. It's all arranged.

JAN. Gonna be a great night — but this heat!

PAUL. Yeah well, that's in our favour. I mean, passion throbs with the thermometer. Bints, the inside of their thighs will be sticky with sweat. Lubberly. O yeah. They'll be going mad with passion in this heat.

JAN. Will they?

PAUL. No doubt about it. Reminds them of their Jamaican heritage. All that. Down by the railway viaducts, poking them — they'll think they're out on the beach in Barbados.

JAN. Bet none of them have been to Barbados.

PAUL. That's nothing to do with it. It's in their sub-conscious, 'cause they're black, see. Bung them a couple of vodka coconut milk cocktails and they're away. Beat of the old Bob Marley and they can't keep their arse still.

JAN. I'll take me hat off.

PAUL. Good thinking.

JAN *takes off his hat.*

Very punk.

JAN. Well, what do we do then?

PAUL. Meet them here, this street corner. My one is definitely bringing one for you.

JAN. Definitely?

PAUL. That was the deal.

JAN. She send a photo?

PAUL. Sent a photo of herself. She didn't send one of her mate, though.

JAN. She's your one?

PAUL (*with a photo*). Yeah. All mine, you lucky girl.

JAN. Let's have a look.

PAUL. Here (*He hands* JAN *the machine photo.*)

JAN. O yeah, O yeah. Looks a bit spotty but —

PAUL. Spotty?

JAN. A bit.

PAUL. I thought they was freckles.

JAN. Maybe they're freckles, O yeah — they're freckles.

PAUL. Might be spots . . .

JAN. Coloured, and all.

PAUL. 'Course she's coloured, that's the whole point.

JAN. I meant the photo.

PAUL. O yeah.

JAN. Which one was she?

PAUL. O yeah well, see — I'm not **quite sure.** I got a bit mixed up. I wrote to a lot of them, see. (*He opens Time Out.*) The ones with the biro squiggles, I wrote to all of them. But I got some of the replies and the **photos** mixed up, didn't I.

I mean, the number who wrote back — I thought it was Christmas!

JAN. Lots of letters, I never get no letters. Blokes in the barracks all get a letter now and again but . . . don't even get a letter from me Uncle Harold.

PAUL. I tell you, the postman who come to me — needed a bleeding articulated lorry. I've narrowed it down. She's either (*He reads:*) 'Virgo widow from Hackney, 28, who misses male company for dancing and mutual pleasure and vegetarian meals' or she's '25, music teacher who likes yoga, Bob Marley and is slowly sinking into a morass of self destruction.' She's warm and sensitive.

JAN. But these are in the magazine?

PAUL. Yeah. That was the idea — have a crack at these. Save money, no need to put an advert in for us. Spoke to her on the blower when she sent her number and said she liked me photo and said I must be Scorpio and a bit kinky. That's the other thing. If we have a nosh later — don't.

JAN. I'm starving.

PAUL. She says she can only be mutual if I'm heavily into macrobiotic grub. Her mate might be the same.

JAN. And she said meet outside a chip shop?

Pause.

PAUL. On the other hand, she might be 'lively exciting bi-sexual are you similar?' (*He laughs, pockets the magazine.*) I think it must be her, since she's bringing her mate. You and me, her and her mate, tonight — once the Carnival gets going, dancing in the streets to the Reggae, two spade bints, tank them up, then back to their place, four of us, getting the old sheets screwed up — here, that fucking skin rash of yours ain't contagious is it?

JAN. Nar. Wish it was.

PAUL. Charming!

JAN. If it was, wouldn't be going across the pond tomorrow, would I . . .

Pause.

PAUL. Cheer up, look happy for God's sake. Carnival. Bit of joy.

JAN. Yeah. Quiet though, init. I thought there'd be thousands of people.

PAUL. Oh, there will be, later.

JAN. And the shops all boarded up . . .

PAUL. All that bother last year, see.

JAN. Definitely meeting them here?

PAUL. This road, opposite the chip shop, by the pub, chip shop, pub. Right place.

JAN. Hard getting here. They re-routed the bus.

PAUL. For the procession. Oh, it's gonna be great. Limbo dancing under the motors and cha-chaing round the parking meters. All that.

JAN. What's she called then?

PAUL. Rosie. Nice name, in't it.

JAN. It's a great name.

PAUL. For Christ's sake Jan cheer up a bit. Bit of happiness. They're probably sussing us out. Look happy otherwise you'll scare them to death.

JAN. There's been a lot.

PAUL. Eh?

JAN. Just saying, there's been a lot of deaths. Over there. The troubled province. (*Pause.*) Troubled province, carelessness.

PAUL *is pacing, looking for the girls.*

Carelessness. The sarge says it's all down to carelessness. If you ain't careless, you're all right. What us lads have got to do is put a ring of steel round the city. Ring of steel. That's what the veterans say. Ring of steel. There's this old bloke, seen a lot of action. O yeah, a lot — Aden, Cyprus. He says: There's nothing like a ring of steel round the city. Like Johnny Turk. That's what knackered him. Ring of steel round Nicosia and it was all over. You arf pick up a lot from these old campaigners. O yeah. Should hear what they say about the Micks. O dear, make you laugh. In the NAAFI. Jokes about the Micks. O yeah. They ain't got a good word to say for them. Not a real war, they say. Not all this bombs in the High Street and snipers. Have to watch out for the snipers. Have to watch out for the snipers. Snipers, they're the lowest of the low.

Disgusting. See, there's a lot of snipers over there. Cross the pond. Lowest of the low. Snipers are. See, you think I'm just standing here on the Portobello Road, right? Waiting for our bi-sexual black bints, right?

PAUL. So many bints. (*He waves.*) Nar, can't be ours or they'd have waved back. (*He shouts.*) Rosie! (*Pause.*) She ain't Rosie. Or Lindy.

JAN. But I'm not looking at the bints though. O no, no way. That'd be careless.

PAUL. O yeah?

JAN. See, what I'm doing is . . . I'm scouring the high vantage points. Look at me, look at me. Right. What am I looking at?

Pause.

PAUL. The chip shop.

JAN. Wrong! I *look* like I'm looking at the chip shop but I ain't. I'm scouring the high vantage points. The roofs. There's a Silver Jubilee flag and a TV aerial on the chip shop roof, right?

PAUL. Right.

JAN. Don't miss a thing. I don't. Develops like an eighth sense. Up here, behind me, on the roof. 'To Let' sign in the third window along.

PAUL. So what?

JAN. Did you see me turn round to look up there and see it?

PAUL. Nar . . .

JAN. There you are, see. Extra sense. Scouring the high vantage points.

PAUL. Brilliant, fucking brilliant.

JAN. Your life's in your eyes.

PAUL. What?

JAN (*during this speech he becomes hysterical*). Sarge says, in a little chat before our twenty-four hour embarkation leave, he says he was right proud of us, couldn't fault us lads. He said we'll all come back safe and sound because we've got our basics right. Use our eyes. Our lives in our eyes. These snipers, they're the lowest of the low. When the other fellers come back, whoosh. That's what they talk about more than the — well, they talk about the bombs and the ambushes, and . . . it's terrible these kids, look like angels, but fucking chucking bombs and . . . But it's the snipers. I've talked to a couple of the lads who've come back. They've tried to keep us apart. I mean they don't really like the lads who've come back talking to the lads who are going out there. but all this sniper talk. O dear. There's a couple of our lads, I mean, seriously, talk about snipers and they have to get up and leave the table. They really literally shit themselves. Watery shits. Don't even know they're doing it. Makes your stomach heave, in a knot. Just talking to you about it, I really feel that I could go to the lavatory like, could do with a good shit, just talking about the snipers. Christ, really does make your stomach do a somersault, the thought of those fucking snipers sitting up on those fucking roofs with their fucking Commie guns just picking off decent fucking Brits, decent lads, just for the fucking fun of fucking shooting the fucking . . .

JAN *is crying.*
PAUL *is horrified. Doesn't know what to do.*
JAN *heaves and pants and wipes his eyes.*

PAUL. Hey, calm down son, calm down.

JAN. Bastards.

PAUL. Yeah.

JAN. Bloody up there, behind the chimneys or something. Bastards.

PAUL. Not here. Not here in Notting Hill for Christ's sake.

JAN. Right. But. O. Bit tense, you know.

PAUL. That's only natural, only natural, in't it.

JAN. Yeah. Arf going to the lav a lot nowadays. Since they give us the embarkation date. Bloody lost half a stone, ain't I. O well, bit tense.

PAUL. You'll be all right, son. 'Course you will. I mean, you've really impressed me. You have. This extra sense lark. I mean I don't normally say nothing about it when I'm impressed.

JAN. Nar, you don't.

PAUL. Takes a lot to impress me. I ain't exactly gushing with compliments.

JAN. Nar, I've always said that about you.

PAUL. I tell you something. That thing you said, what was up there on the roof of the chip shop. I mean, that really did impress me.

JAN. Did it really?

PAUL. Honest, I couldn't figure it out. How you'd noticed. I really didn't clock how you'd seen up there.

JAN. Well, it's a knack.

PAUL. You've sure got it.

JAN. Like a skill.

PAUL. Very clever.

JAN. Extra sense.

PAUL. You're telling me.

JAN. Been a sniper up there, he wouldn't have known I'd clocked him.

PAUL. Yeah, and you would have just whipped up your gun and fucking blown the bleeder into kingdom come.

JAN. Yeah. After I'd got the okay.

PAUL. Eh?

JAN. Well, see — can't just shoot a bloke 'cause he's up on the roof.

PAUL. Fucking sniper?

JAN. Ah see, got to know he's a sniper.

PAUL. If he's on a . . . 'high vantage point'.

JAN. But, got to get the okay. He might not be a sniper.

PAUL. What's he doing on the fucking roof then?

JAN. Might be a chimney sweep.

PAUL. With a shooter in his hand?

JAN. Ah, but it might be a stick to clean out a bit of the chimney that's blocked up.

PAUL. Come off it.

JAN. No, it's orders. Can't shoot, till he shoots at me.

PAUL. Let him shoot you?

JAN. Nar, take preventive actions, don't I. Hide in a doorway. It's all right. It's err . . . you know.

PAUL. Oh yeah.

JAN. I mean, it ain't as simple as you'd think. Ireland, it's all a bit complicated.

PAUL. Yeah, sure.

JAN. It's not a normal war, see.

PAUL. Sure, I see that.

JAN. Have to look like you're okay. Not let on that you're . . . you know, a bit . . .

PAUL. Bit tense?

JAN. Bit tense, like.

PAUL. Yeah, but — it's like anything. Init. Before you go. But you know, once you're there!

JAN. Yeah.

PAUL. A month's time. I bet I get a postcard from you all cheerful. You'll be wondering what you was worrying about.

JAN. Yeah, yeah.

PAUL. Tonight. Last night in —

JAN. In London. Before I come back.

PAUL. Before you come back. Make it a night to remember.

JAN. Yeah. I'm really glad you've fixed up these black birds. I've always wanted to fuck a spade, before I . . . you know, go.

PAUL. Sure.

JAN. The old timers, they say there's nothing like spade women.

PAUL. You bet. Thought we'd have made contact by now. What is the time?

JAN. 20.14.

PAUL. Eh?

JAN. In civilian jargon, nearly quarter past eight.

PAUL (shouts). Rosie, it's me. (Pause.) Ain't her.

JAN. O yeah. Funny, you'd have thought the streets'd be full of people.

PAUL. Getting dark. Tonight, once it gets dark, that's when the fireworks'll start.

LOUIS *enters and addresses the audience. Just light on* LOUIS *who wears a silk shirt, a white suit and smokes a cigar.*

LOUIS. Tonight . . . after dark . . . when it really begins. They'll be coming in their hundreds, thousands, on trains and buses, on bikes, in cars, walking, running . . . for the masquerade. The sky lit up with fireworks. Dancing in the streets. Air buzzing with rum and blue beat. And laughter. O yeah. When times get hard, all the more reason for the masquerade. Like it goes back in history, don't it? Like, however poor you are, well — come the Carnival and you can play being a rich man. You can dress in the finest clothes there's ever been. For weeks, they've been making the costumes. The butterflies — wait till you see the butterfly men! Me mum and me sister and these other ladies, they took over this warehouse for three weeks to make the butterflies. Huge, huge. Like for the great — release! Like it's back home, here in the streets of London town. And everytime anyone says, well things ain't good and things are gonna get worse, maybe one day, I go home, back to Kingston — Come the Carnival they say — no way! We make it happen here, man. Just two days, two days, that's all we need. Even the cavemen and 'at, at Stonehenge and all that, all them millions of years ago, they had their carnivals. You've gotta have your dream. The fantasy, know what I mean. In the streets, all come together. Blacks and whites and the Chinese and the Indians, and we all . . . get drunk on the happiness in the streets. Oh yeah.

Lights to full.
JAN *and* PAUL *approach.*

PAUL. Bloody hell — it's Louis.

LOUIS. Paul! Hey Jan, you did it.

JAN. Yeah, I did it.

LOUIS. You joined up.

JAN. The Regulars. Yeah, I joined up.

LOUIS. You've come to the Carnival.

JAN. Last few hours. Before embarkation. I'm going to Belfast in the morning.

PAUL. Bloody Shaft!

LOUIS. Best suit.

PAUL. Doing all right, eh?

LOUIS. Real good.

PAUL. Got a job?

LOUIS. Yeah, refrigeration. And, got a motor. Only a van, but me own transport, like.

JAN. Better than the factory.

LOUIS. Army's better than the factory.

JAN. Yeah.

LOUIS. And where are you now, Paul?

PAUL. Well, went back to the factory. For a bit. Tide meself over. Bit of a cock up. Joined Securicor, didn't I.

LOUIS. You was a security man.

PAUL. Found I had a bit of talent for it. Started off casual like, on the marches in Lewisham, oh they was great. So, took it up full time. With Securicor instead of the Front. Bloody cosh, they give me. Sitting in the back of the old tank. This great Alsatian. I'll go back to them, when me eye clears up, you know.

LOUIS. Your eye?

PAUL. Bit out of sorts. (*He laughs.*) Should have gone to the quack about it straight away. The glass had got in the retina, hadn't it. All the while fucking it up and I didn't know. Right shock it was when one day . . .

Pause.

LOUIS. I'm really sorry about that Paul, really sorry.

PAUL. Good job I started off with two eh?

LOUIS. Well, you're really going to enjoy things tonight.

PAUL. Funny seeing you like this Louis mate. All so real cool, like.

LOUIS. Well . . . you know . . .

PAUL. Not much of the old Jimmy Dean about him now, eh Jan?

LOUIS. Everyone grows up.

PAUL. That's true. Some of the pranks we got up to, eh?

LOUIS. Yeah.

PAUL. That motor! Cup final. Motor and now you've got one yourself.

LOUIS. Only a van, with the job, like.

PAUL. Still ,better than nothing.

LOUIS. Anyone still at the factory that I knew?

PAUL. Few, few. Lot of kids there now. Don't care about nothing. Not interested in the overtime so us old hands do all right. Mr Baker died.

LOUIS. He died?

PAUL. Had a stroke, didn't he. Just before Christmas. Then he copped it. Best way, otherwise he'd have just been a vegetable.

JAN. Best way.

PAUL. He was the only one who could keep those bloody young tearaways in hand. Now, they don't give a fuck about anyone.

JAN. We was just wondering, like — the procession. Where it comes.

PAUL. Yeah, I mean. Is it this road, like?

LOUIS. Nar. Look, you come with me and I'll show you.

PAUL. Meeting some bints, in't we.

LOUIS. Fantastic. Then you bring them.

JAN. They haven't got here yet.

LOUIS. O well, when they do.

PAUL. Sure.

LOUIS. Glad everything worked out for the both of you.

PAUL. Certainly worked out for you, son.

LOUIS. Yeah, moved here, you know. Like, all the family here now. It's okay, like real close.

JAN. That's nice.

LOUIS. She's sure going to miss you while you're away.

JAN. Who?

LOUIS. Your girlfriend.

JAN. O well, she's not a regular, like.

LOUIS. Be nice to have a girl though, won't it. You got a photo?

JAN. I'll ask her for a photo, if we get on like.

LOUIS. Get on?

JAN. Well, err. (*Pause.*) Made contact, Paul has and . . .

PAUL. Pair of spade bints. Great to have a spade.

JAN. Never had a spade, I ain't.

PAUL. All right, aren't they. Things they get up to.

LOUIS. O . . . (*His reaction.*)

JAN. What the blokes who've been abroad say, about nigger tarts.

LOUIS. Great . . .

PAUL. Can't get enough, go on all night, that right?

LOUIS. Sure, all blacks — sex mad.

PAUL. Fantastic.

LOUIS. You know niggers. Fuck like animals.

PAUL. That's what I heard.

LOUIS. Because of the jungle. Like apes. And the ladies, nymphos.

PAUL (*to* JAN). What did I tell you son? Once they get here, oh yeah.

LOUIS. O yeah?

PAUL. So I've heard, these negresses. O dear. Make it sound like you need to do Canadian Airman's exercises to get in training for them. Bloody contortionists.

LOUIS. You cunt. (*He turns to go.*)

JAN. Louis, what's the matter?

LOUIS. You fucking pair of . . .

JAN. No offence. Just saying like, neither of us have had a nigger.

LOUIS. Go some place else. Fuck a dog, just the same.

PAUL. Oi oi. Bit oity toity, ain't you. Integration, in't it. I'll report you to the Race Relations Board.

LOUIS. Disgusting — bastards. (*Again he turns to go.*)

PAUL (*to* JAN). What's up with him.

JAN. Dunno. Louis, what's the matter?

LOUIS. If you don't know, it's a waste of my time telling you.

He walks away.
JAN *and* PAUL *follow.*

PAUL. Tell us where you and your mob'll be hanging out and as soon as these bints turn up we'll shoot round to you.

LOUIS. Drop dead.

JAN. Louis, it's us. Your old mates.

LOUIS. You talk about black girls like . . .

JAN. They don't mind.

PAUL. 'Course they don't mind. That's what those bloody adverts are for. Bloody knocking shop.

JAN. And me last night before embarkation.

LOUIS. You got them in an advert?

JAN. In Time Out, yeah.

LOUIS (*incredulous, then laughs*). Got them in an advert. Lonely hearts club band? Lonely hearts, oh man but that's pathetic. That's the funniest thing I ever heard, you mean you — in an advert. They're for wankers, they're for the pathetic old shits. An advert for a bint, that's too too much. (*He goes, laughing.*)

PAUL. Flash bastard. Who's he think he's laughing at?

JAN. He thought it was funny.

PAUL. What?

JAN. Suppose it is. A bit.

PAUL. Cocky spade. What's up with him? Gone a bit bloody flash. Bit bloody holy nigger all of a sudden. What's he think this is? It's Notting Hill, it's London in't it. Ain't Jamaica. Taking the piss out of us. And you, you in Her Majesty's uniform.

JAN. Yeah but . . . still, never mind eh?

PAUL. I do mind. I bloody do mind. He was one of us a year ago. Now pissed off, all niggers together. Piss off white men. That's nice in't it, after all I've done for him. There's two kinds of spades I hate. Spades who act like they ain't spades and spades who're cocky 'cause they are spades.

JAN. He's become a real cocky spade.

PAUL. I'll have him.

JAN. We'll go somewhere else. Cool down and . . . go up West.
Instead. I just wanna do something, you know. Something to
remember before tomorrow. Night to remember.

PAUL. I'll have him.

JAN. Shall I tell you something?

PAUL. I can still hear him laughing.

JAN. I'll tell you something.

PAUL. I'll fucking have him.

JAN. See, the regulars —

PAUL. Eh?

JAN. In me Regiment.

PAUL. I told you you was fucking mad to sign up.

JAN. Didn't want the factory all me life. Anyway, all them on
the dole. Me Uncle Harold told me he'd heard they was going
to start conscription. He said: 'Join the Regular Army and
you'll be head and shoulders above the conscripts when they
start conscription.'

PAUL. Stupid prat.

JAN. Yeah, well. I wanted the catering corps, didn't I? He said
so long as there's people, there's food. Get into catering and
be all right. Lying sods, they said they'd have me in the
catering corps. When there was a vacancy. How come I'm
going to Belfast then? With a gun?

PAUL. Lonely hearts club . . . pathetic. See the way he looked
at me? Coming to something, in't it. Bloody spades laughing
at you. 'Cause you're white. I'll report him to the Race
Relations Board — or kick his head in.

JAN. Them stewards, they look really hard, like — real hard.

PAUL. That one of your skills? Knowing when someone's
really hard? One kick in the right place — no-one laughs at me.
Climb up on the chip shop roof, drop fucking bricks on the
spade's head. That's what I feel like doing.

JAN. I'm a trained killer. I know all the places to go for to kill.
The nerves to strike. Bite the jugular, cigarette in the eyeball,
break a back on me knee . . .

PAUL. That right?

Pause.

JAN. Destroy the enemy.

PAUL. Enemy ain't he!

JAN. They meant Micks. The IRA and all them.

PAUL. He laughed at you!

JAN. Yeah, but I mean . . . he knew, like — the adverts.

PAUL. I wouldn't be seen dead looking through them adverts
for meself. I did it for you, son. Give you a night out in the
city to remember.

Pause.

A black bint. Wank over the memory in the barracks. Under
the blankets when the lights are out. Winter nights in Belfast,
need something.

JAN. Don't go on about Belfast for Christ's sake.

PAUL. Snipers'll be there, looking for you. (*Silence.*) He laughed
at us, cocky bastard. Spades, got it made. At school, all
mates. On the dole, all mates. Then they disappear, you know.
Wonder why that is? All mates and suddenly . . . They
disappear into their Reggae clubs and . . . never mix with us . . .
the factory . . . sit at different tables in the canteen . . . a
million miles apart . . . (*Pause.*) All that rhythm . . . all that
joy . . . all their big white teeth smiling . . . flashing in the
dark . . . all their 'anything goes', why don't misery choke
them? Louis, laughing at me. He wouldn't have been laughing
if he'd seen us on the march in Lewisham the other week, mate.

Pause.

Later, get him on his own . . . on his own . . . Just another
mugging, it'll be. They'll think, cops'll think, it was the
spades. Notting Hill. The Carnival. All the fault of the spades.
Never know it was us. Make him bleed. Shouldn't have
laughed at us. Spot him. Find him. Have him.

Pause.

JAN. But be reasonable. I mean to say —

PAUL. What?

Silence.

JAN. Last night, I want . . . here . . . go up West and me in me
uniform, really pull. I'll put me hat back on. Would have
been nice, bi-sexual black bints, oh yeah, but it ain't worked
out.

PAUL. Few drinks, get tanked up. You want to be part of
something. No family, not the army, and this . . . Carnival.
Won't let you be part of that. We're not part of nothing.
Nothing. We're . . . nothing. Let him laugh at you?

JAN. Nar?

PAUL. Let snipers laugh at you?

JAN. Nar.

PAUL. No-one laughs at you.

JAN. No.

PAUL. You hate people laughing at you.

JAN. Yeah . . . I know I do. Know I do . . .

PAUL *goes.* JAN *alone, just the light on him.*

JAN. They laughed at me mum . . . destroyed her. They took
away her bowels, to stop it spreading. The doctors did. They
gave her a plastic bag, she hated it — the bag to urinate in.
She hated it, she said it was like having a bath wearing a life
belt. She used to sing in the pub, by the flats. She wanted a
garden. We never had one in the flats. Never lived on the
ground, me mum didn't. The pub had a garden. Sit there,
drinking her Dubonnet and lemonade. She used to sing at
the pub at nights sometimes. They had turns and she'd get up
and sing. Even when she was very ill. And one Saturday night,
she had this . . . she had this lovely voice, beautiful. When she
sang 'Goodnight Irene', old women cried. She was a legend,
her voice. (*He sings:*)

Irene, goodnight, Irene goodnight I'll see you in my dreams.

Pause. He begins to cry.

And this Saturday night, they had this dwarf comic. He told
tall stories and jokes, made me mum laugh. He said — see,
there used to be a lot of blacks in there, and so he told jokes
about the blacks. They liked them, I mean — well, they had to
like them.

Pause.

And when he went off the stage, they never took off the
microphone. And it was still there, only about three and a
half feet from the ground. They asked for a song and me
Uncle Harold, he said to me mum: 'Give us a song, Elsie'.
And the other people, they all said: 'Give us a song Elsie'.
And she said: 'O no, I can't.' And then they all started

chanting: 'Elsie, give us a song.' And the man on the piano, called Charles, he started playing the beginning of 'Goodnight Irene' 'cause it was like her signature tune and eventually she got up and she was very overcome because of all the warmth and the pub was nice, with warmth and friendship. And she stood up and the drummer gave her the hand microphone and still they forgot the dwarf's microphone which was still standing right in front of my mum. And she put up her hand to stop everyone cheering and the piano player asked for hush and my mum said: 'I'm very overcome to know you all cared for me 'cause of the collection from the pub to send me flowers when I had my unfortunate operation . . .' And she was very err . . . moved. Moved. And in the quiet, there was this sound . . . this noise. Coming out of the loudspeakers. Because the dwarf's microphone was still switched on . . . it was standing about waist height to my mother. The sound of gushing water. The microphone picked up the sound of my mum passing water into her plastic bag. Everyone could hear it. Through the loud speakers, the sound went on and some people they . . . they . . . (*Pause.*) And some people, some of the people . . . (*Pause.*) Laughed. They laughed.

He stops crying. Long silence.

That night at home, she got up out of bed and went to the bathroom and drank a pint of bleach. Which killed her. (*Pause.*) After that, it was very quiet at home. I went two nights every week to the Cadets and then . . . I signed up. I don't . . . talk about it much. When I had the medical, I didn't tell them about my mum . . . I thought it best to say 'natural causes'.

He stands there silently.
Lights from a lamppost, a scream. PAUL has LOUIS on the ground and is kicking him. There is blood on LOUIS' white jacket.

LOUIS. Hey Paul, why why?

PAUL. Black cunt.

LOUIS. Why the −

JAN moves in horror towards them.

JAN. For Christ's sake − leave him alone.

PAUL. Black bastard.

LOUIS. Why are you doing this to me?

PAUL. 'Cause, I'm doing it.

JAN *tries to restrain* PAUL.

JAN. No Paul, please. No trouble. I'm going to Belfast in the morning.

PAUL. There'll be trouble there.

JAN. No trouble. I embark at 16.00 hours . . . so there mustn't be any trouble.

PAUL. Kick his head in . . . get arrested, then they won't send you. Black shit. Flash nigger, you've made it boy, flash nigger.

LOUIS. I made a go of things, I worked hard.

PAUL. Then how come it worked for you and not for me?

LOUIS. Because I tried things instead of just smashing them.

PAUL. I tried and all.

JAN. I don't want to go to Belfast.

PAUL. Don't want the factory. Securicor wouldn't have me as a driver 'cause of me eye.

JAN. See Louis, they chucked him out of Securicor when they found out about his eye. Leave him Paul, you'll kill him. I only wanted a nice night out with some black bi-sexuals.

PAUL. Why have we stopped being together?

LOUIS. Paul, please . . . I'm hurting.

JAN. Paul, you'll kill him. . . You're pissed, you've gone berserk. (*To* LOUIS.) Sorry about this, he's a bit fed up. (*To* PAUL.) For God's sake, all blood and snot and broken bits of teeth . . . he's bleeding. (*To* LOUIS.) I'll get an ambulance. Embarkation for me tomorrow . . . in Christ . . . just a couple of hours . . . There'll be snipers on the roofs. Up there, there's a Jubilee flag on the chip shop roof, don't it look nice? I only wanted to be a pastry chef. I thought, better than the factory and me Uncle Harold said as long as there's food there's people and you shouldn't have laughed. I'd have killed you only I've got to go to Belfast and they wouldn't let me go if I was a murderer 'cause you have to ask permission to kill.

PAUL. Kill him . . . kill him . . .

LOUIS. Me dad said, no matter how bad it is, you can take it boy.

JAN. I never knew me dad properly.

PAUL. Bleed nigger, bleed.

LOUIS. Ah, ah . . .

PAUL. Keeeeeelllllll . . .

JAN. I dunno why they're sending me to Belfast . . . I've got to kick you Louis so they arrest me and I don't have to go.

Police siren, blue flashing lights. PAUL *runs off.*

LOUIS. Run away Jan, run away, fuck off.

JAN *kicks* LOUIS.
JAN *turns to the audience.*

JAN. You'd better arrest me, I'm mad and very violent.

LOUIS. He didn't do nothing, it was the other one.

JAN. It was me.

LOUIS. Weren't you Jan.

JAN. It was me. I'll kick him again to prove it.

JAN *with reluctance kicks* LOUIS. *Pleads to audience.*

LOUIS. He only did that so you'll arrest him and he won't go tomorrow.

JAN. You'd better lock me up tonight, please. For a long time. I'll come quietly. If you promise to lock me up. Lock me up. I'm violent. I'm a trained killer. So you'd better lock me up. Please . . . please . . . (*He smiles.*) You're going to lock me up for a long time?

LOUIS. Not him, the other one.

JAN *kicks* LOUIS *savagely.*

LOUIS. He's only kicking me so you won't let him kill someone else.

JAN. See, I did it all. I'm a trained killer. Lock me up. To protect myself . . . and society from everything you've done to me. 'Cause, 'cause . . . otherwise I'll do it back. To you. Worse

He holds out his hands for the handcuffs.
Blackout

End of play.